The Watchtower and the Cross

The Watchtower and the Cross

A Journey into Faith

D. A. SHANE

RESOURCE *Publications* • Eugene, Oregon

THE WATCHTOWER AND THE CROSS
A Journey into Faith

Copyright © 2024 D. A. Shane. All rights reserved. Except for brief quotations in critical publications or reviews, no part of this book may be reproduced in any manner without prior written permission from the publisher. Write: Permissions, Wipf and Stock Publishers, 199 W. 8th Ave., Suite 3, Eugene, OR 97401.

Resource Publications
An Imprint of Wipf and Stock Publishers
199 W. 8th Ave., Suite 3
Eugene, OR 97401

www.wipfandstock.com

PAPERBACK ISBN: 979-8-3852-0993-4
HARDCOVER ISBN: 979-8-3852-0994-1
EBOOK ISBN: 979-8-3852-0995-8

05/15/24

Unless otherwise noted, all scriptures are from the 1899 Douay-Rheims Bible, public domain.

For Maude, my editor and my everything.

"Come and hear, all ye that fear God, and I will tell you what great things he hath done for my soul" (Psalm 65:16).

Contents

Chapter 1: Under the Sign of the Watchtower — 1

Chapter 2: Life Along the Watchtower — 13

Chapter 3: Dedication, Rebellion, and New Gods — 31

Chapter 4: Rebel Without a Prayer — 45

Chapter 5: The Darkness Shattered — 60

Chapter 6: The Outlines of Reality — 77

Chapter 7: Christ's Church, the Devil's Dogs, and the Unmaking of a Family — 92

Chapter 8: Adventure and the Burning Path — 109

Chapter 9: The Household of God — 123

Chapter 10: Under the Sign of the Cross — 134

Appendix: The Trinity for Jehovah's Witnesses — 151

Bibliography — 153

Chapter 1

Under the Sign of the Watchtower

I was born at Baptist Hospital in Nashville, Tennessee, in the late eighties. The building itself is modernist and dull, but it's a good hospital. Recently it was bought out by a Catholic health care group and named after a saint. Crucifixes went up where empty crosses had hung before. My children were born there, after the institution's conversion. The years between their births and mine saw another conversion to the Catholic fold as well. That, along with many other twists and turns, is the story I want to tell.

The beginning of that story starts with the realization of a lifelong dream by my father. He had built a little cottage for his new family on some farmland on Tennessee's Highland Rim, land he had bought jointly with his father and brother. He built it with his own two hands—he was a self-taught carpenter, and generally a master of any mechanical art he put his mind to. I was not to be raised in that home (though I spent some time there in utero) because of several family disagreements that scuttled my grandfather's original plan for a shared homestead. One of those disagreements was over something that will form the background of most of this story: the Jehovah's Witness faith (also known by the metonym "Watchtower," the name of their flagship publication). In this case, it was my uncle's lapse in the practice of that faith.

My uncle stayed on and farmed that land, though, and has been there ever since. His stability has acted as a subtle rebuke to my parents' wanderlust. Unlike him, my parents were seeking metaphorically greener pastures in one of the growing suburban towns near Nashville. There we rented one side of a little duplex not far from the center of town. Most of my earliest memories center on that half-side of a house and the sprawling "edge city" nearby, where the mall and other stores were.

Don't get the idea that because I've talked about farming and building houses with bare hands that I lived any kind of different life materially from most American kids. In fact, besides the Southern accents that mostly filled the air around me, you'd be hard-pressed to find much else that differed from the typical picture of a kid growing up in the nineties. Perhaps that helps explain a lifelong desire for "authenticity," a common trait among many Millennials. I won't try to enhance my authenticity credentials in this narrative by portraying my childhood as idyllically rural or stereotypically rustic or anything. It was partly this "boring" normalcy that impelled me to seek out the deeper things later in life.

In utterly typical fashion, I was given a Super Nintendo at age 4 or 5, on which I eagerly played *Donkey Kong Country* and *Super Mario World*. As I think happens very often with more intellectually inclined youngsters these days, video games took on a great importance to me. I do remember playing outside, though, on a playset and sandbox my dad constructed. My only sibling, a sister, was born five years after me. I was a particularly jealous, exclusionary big brother, something I regret now. One time my toddling sister was attempting to follow me outside. With the pretense of "protecting" her by keeping her inside, I slammed the screen door hard in her face. Her tiny fingers had managed to establish a beachhead on the door frame, though, and so were flattened. We had to rush to the hospital, but apparently the malleability of babies' bones prevented any breakage.

I don't have many memories of young childhood. The only memories I have of religious services from this age are of one time being jerked up for a whupping during a meeting and another time being told that I had to stop drawing and coloring during the service. The religious activity I recall most explicitly is my dad reading a Bible story book to me, a retelling of much of Scripture for children by the Jehovah's Witnesses. A lot of the mental pictures I have of biblical stories probably derive from the illustrations in this book.

The town/suburb we lived in was getting a bit pricey for people like us even back in those days. You would probably think anyone writing a navel-gazing memoir like this would be from a bookish family, maybe upper middle-class, but that brings me to another aspect of life in the Jehovah's Witness (JW) organization (which, by the way, was usually just referred to as "the organization" by the members—part of the strange molding of minds via vocabulary that they do). The JWs are anti-higher education. Going to a four-year college is strongly discouraged.

The obvious downside to this policy is that in a post-industrial economy, your members are probably going to be barred from most of the decent paying jobs. You could imagine this situation leading to frustration and burnout among an increasingly overworked and underpaid, proletarianized membership. But from what I've observed, there are actually several counterbalancing benefits that have helped keep the policy in place. One is the obvious benefit of having more ignorant followers: education of course has the tendency to make people question things, which is none too helpful in any authoritarian system, much less one based on a "truth" that frequently changes. It also helps, when you're teaching people novel conclusions about history, archaeology, and science, if they've had as little exposure to these disciplines as possible. Second, people with little in the way of material success are generally less attached to possessions or status and so better devotees in the spiritual life. A skeptic would call it "the opium of the masses"; a believer might reference a camel and the eye of a needle. But even most folks in the latter camp would take issue with deliberately creating a membership made up of the undereducated.

So, since my parents had forsaken higher education for "the highest education in the universe"[1] (despite my mom being valedictorian of her high school), they were employed in blue collar industries. In no way am I ashamed or embarrassed by that fact. The pretentious obsession with make-work white collar "careers" in this country is one of the greatest indicators of our general unseriousness as a nation. No society could (or should even want to) exist without many people who work with their hands. Many European countries understand this and privilege the manual trades in like manner to professional pursuits. But here, the land of pioneers and frontiersmen, the land built by physical courage and technical ingenuity, we shunt the tradesmen and laborers aside, making no provision for them in our policies or space for them in our cities. To me it could only be class or cultural malice, the malice implicit in an epithet like "deplorable" or a useless commonplace like "learn to code."

Why we had been living where we lived in the first place, I'm not sure. We didn't have roots in that community. My father's line was from Nashville and Davidson County, having been off the farm for a couple generations. Momma teased him that he had enjoyed a *Leave it to Beaver*-type

---

1. This was an oft-repeated catchphrase at a district convention years ago.

upbringing, and from what I can tell, he did: my grandfather was a solidly middle-class salesman who provided a typical mid-century white suburban existence for his family. But I should mention that this idyllic picture was only a generation removed from the Nashville housing projects (where my grandfather spent part of his childhood). It sounds cliché, but there was a great deal of bootstrap-pulling that went into getting our family into that comfortable position.

My mother's family, on the other hand, was from a sparsely populated county. Tennessee used to put your county's population size ranking on each license plate, so that a car with a number two ranking (Davidson County, second largest county by population in the state) and one with a number ninety-five ranking (i.e., the smallest county in the state) could be seen meeting up during my parents' courtship, which was amusing to them. I don't really know what my maternal family's relative socio-economic position was within their community, though I don't think anyone in that county, then or now, was particularly well-off. I do know she recounts many experiences that would be familiar to people growing up in the rural South of that time—running around barefoot outside and getting hookworm, for instance. My grandfather even remembers a time without electricity, back in the early forties before TVA came in and gave the region access to modern amenities. When it got dark, the day was over. He even remembers tales from the oldest folks in the county about how the Tennessee River ran red with blood after the Battle of Shiloh, which was fought not too far away.

Anyway, I say all that to say, my mother had wanted to leave her remote hometown for a long time, and my father had been wanting to get to one for nearly as long, and so much of the next fifteen years was spent working out a compromise location. That started with the great land deal and plan of settlement on the family homestead and somehow mutated into that Nashville suburb. After five years there, however, the lay of the land had changed once more and my mother's attitude toward her home area had softened. It was decided that we would move a county over from Mom's birthplace, so as to be close (but not too close) to her folks.

Dad worked in the mobile home business, so there were deals to be had with that type of housing. We put a little single-wide on a piece of land outside town while Dad set about building his second house, a two-story American Vernacular, tucked away in the woods at the end of a dirt road. At the trailer I again recall my Super Nintendo but also playing in the creek out back and being surprised by all the noises frogs could make. Dad would give me small cleaning jobs to do at the new house's construction site. He always put me to work at something, and he steadily increased the load and complexity of work as I grew. This was none too pleasing to me as I got older, until I was grown and realized the great gift he'd given me. As an adult I've been able to see manual labor as something healthy and vivifying and have rarely resented it.

However, though I imbibed an appreciation of labor, I did not absorb the technical skills he sought to transmit to me, which is another regret. I had the chance to learn under one of the greatest master carpenters I'm likely ever to meet, and I took no interest. To me that's one of the greatest tragedies of life, this narrow focus most of us fall into: to feel nothing for all topics and pursuits outside of the small range of trifles that happen to strike one's fancy at a given time. It's almost a negation of life itself. The world is so much greater than any one mind can conceive, full of history and technique and art, and yet we spurn it all as "boring" for the mere fact that our provincial little intellect has fastened on some one or two things. For me, part of wading out into the broad stream of the real life, of the life lived in the light of providence, has been an attempt to broaden my interests. There's not a single petal on the tiniest flower that doesn't merit my attention, interest, and love, just for what it is—just *that* it is!

But many short-sighted tendencies are on display in childhood, and whether children have the capacity for broad-mindedness is a legitimate question. I certainly did not, and so I took no interest at all in picking up my father's craft. Whether the blame falls more to video games or to my abstract, artistic nature, I couldn't say. Above all I loved to draw, and I paid minute attention to the colors and features of various cartoon and comic book characters. In fact my earliest memories of religious service, as I mentioned, were wanting nothing more than to draw and color during the long "meetings" (as services are called) at the "Kingdom Hall" (as the houses of worship are called). But Daddy *would not* let me do it, from the earliest time I can remember. I was to take notes, or to tally up how many times the speaker said "Jehovah" (the translation of the Divine Name the Witnesses insist upon) or "Jesus." Neither of those activities could assuage my boredom for long, which probably explains my memories of being quite dramatically yanked up by my father and taken to the back for a whupping a few times for misbehaving.

Whether you consider these tactics harsh or not, they seem to have had the intended effect. My experience of religion turned serious fairly early, before that of any of my peers. Being a precocious child and a good reader certainly didn't hurt either. I'll briefly lay out how such advancement in the JW religion works. Your first step is to become a publisher, that title probably being in reference to someone who "publishes the good news" (akin to the more familiar "preaching the Gospel"). This entitles you to go in the door-to-door preaching work the Witnesses are so famous for. You can also "give talks," which means delivering speeches before the congregation. These begin as simple readings from Scripture and graduate up to manuscript- and outline-form discourses, but back in the mid-nineties even the lowest tier of talk required an introduction and conclusion framing the Scripture passage in the speaker's own words. Baptism comes after the age of reason but for many not until age fifteen or sixteen. "Making a dedication to Jehovah" in baptism opens up greater avenues of responsibility, the first step being "ministerial servant." The talks a ministerial servant can give are more complex and deal more with procedures and protocols, and they can also give public talks, which are the main Sunday sermons. From the ranks of the ministerial servants will be selected the "elders," which would be the highest rank the average enterprising male JW could hope to attain (ranks above baptized publishers are not open to women). Above elders there are only various types of traveling overseers and the leadership hierarchy at headquarters.

I think I gave my first talk at age six or seven, which is relatively early. My articulate and serious delivery elicited much praise, and I think I was marked out for advancement. I was otherwise normal at this age, since video games and drawing are pretty standard for most boys. When the new house in the woods was finished, I had a ton of forested hills and hollows to roam around on, and I did take advantage of that. My cousins and I, sometimes with Dad's help, would fashion wooden weapons for use out in the field. Daddy loved nature and tried to teach me about the various species of trees, but I didn't pay much attention.

I had a great father. Even from a young age I was somewhat cognizant of how lucky I was. He made every effort to be home with us if at all possible. He even avoided and delayed certain promotions because, as he said, "Then you'd never see me." None of my cousins or friends had a dad as good as mine, and they even told me as much. My father was eminently fair and merciful yet in no way indulgent or lax in disciplining me. Punishment was handled with a cool and level head, and always predictably and consistently. There was no shadow of turning in my father. He spanked me quite a lot (he says maybe too much), but I never had the feeling of being unjustly treated. Other dads would be present or absent, or would fly off the handle one day and barely raise their voice the next. Not my dad.

As good a father as he was, it was surprising to find out that he didn't originally want to be a father. My mother told me that his face dropped when she announced to him she was pregnant with me. That's probably disconcerting or at least surprising to you as well: don't most conservative Christians think of raising a family as a good thing?

Most do, but not the Jehovah's Witnesses. Along with the rest of the Protestant world, the JWs accepted artificial contraception as licit many decades ago. Unlike other Protestants, though, they have made a particular virtue of the child-free life. For some shred of Scriptural backing, they turn to Christ's prediction that in the last days, "blessed are the barren, and the wombs that have not borne" (Luke 23:29). The prophecy is speaking about a calamitous time during which all the natural drives and patterns of life would be disrupted or become burdensome. For the ancient world, children were an unalloyed good, and so to imagine a time where people would say to their children, in effect, "It would be better if you'd never been born!" is a striking image indeed.

However you want to exactly interpret it, the JWs have certainly taken this and run with it. A culture has grown up among them (with the hierarchy's blessing—nothing in that organization takes place without their knowledge or sanction) that frowns upon bearing children. The idea is that, if you truly believe that God is soon to destroy the wicked world and then usher in a paradise earth where death will be no more and faithful ones will be able to have all the kids they ever wanted, then why would you selfishly want to bring kids into this present dysfunctional world? It's looked upon as a kind of materialism, or as a desire born of weakness and vanity because if you were sufficiently zealous for "Kingdom interests," as the phrasing goes, then why wouldn't you redirect those desires and that energy toward preaching and teaching others about your hope, so that they could enjoy the Paradise as well? As my experience will suggest, I think there's also an unspoken fear that having a kid creates the possibility that the child will "reject the truth" (i.e., the JW religion) and therefore be painfully cut off. Why risk it?

So it happens that even though it's not against the rules to have children, the most elite Witnesses will usually avoid it. Traveling overseers (the first rung above an elder) and up are almost solely drawn from the childless—but not the celibate! And here is another important point. JWs also share the Protestant suspicion of the unmarried. It's rare for a bachelor to climb very far in the ranks. When you put these two things together—disdain for procreation, yet marriage as a requirement for promotion—you get what is for all intents and purposes a sacralization of birth control. Enjoying only contraceptive, non-procreative relations becomes the expectation and usually the only thing standing between the couple and the loss of a vaunted position.[2]

My father is a serious, earnest man who's honest to a fault. He lives a consistent, coherent life. If God's representatives on earth suggest to him that raising a family is suboptimal, he's going to try to avoid it. And so that's why he wasn't thrilled when my mother announced to him she was pregnant with me. I guess there's nothing too shocking in that; plenty of people don't want kids. It's more the fact that this man probably thought he was letting down God by having one. The fact that he was such an excellent dad in practice says to me it was deeper in him to want them, or that he was the kind of person suited to raising children and should've wanted them.

So I grew in stature and in the fear of Jehovah under this man's tutelage. In school in our small town, where I attended the first through third grades, I had plenty of friends, despite the fact that I had to absent myself from all activities associated with any holidays or birthdays. In an attempt to alleviate some of the embarrassment of a seven-year-old boy when these types of situations would inevitably arise, at the beginning of every school year my parents would go to the parent-teacher night where they could meet my teacher for the coming year. They would explain that we were Jehovah's Witnesses and that therefore I would need to be excused from certain activities, and they'd hand her a brochure with a baby blue-colored cover that went into all the details about the pagan roots of such celebrations. The idea is that anything borrowed or taken over from pagans is eternally pagan. Based on their reckoning, I guess I assumed just about everything "worldly" (i.e., non-Witness) people did was inadvertently involving them in the worship of ancient deities.

There's a lot going on with this rejection of traditions. You're probably familiar with what might be called the "puritanical" impulse in Protestantism, which led to things like iconoclasm and the banning of Christmas and

---

2. Couples generally have to resign from a headquarters post once they have children. There are obviously logistical and financial reasons that play into this, but the general feeling of children being an imposition and a career-killer inevitably flows from it.

dancing by the congregationalist settlers in New England. JWs not only draw from this well but have their own homegrown tradition of being different for difference's sake. Everyone's heard of Christmas being secretly pagan, but what in the world would possess a religion to ban something like Thanksgiving? The Watchtower's second president, "Judge" J.T. Rutherford, was the one who implemented a lot of the changes that made the Witnesses so unique and for which they would become famous. He reportedly hated women and his own mother so much that he banned Mother's Day.

His stated goal was to make the Witnesses different. How does a tiny upstart sect compete with larger, more established bodies? You've got to stand out from the rest of the pack. A religion that claims to be the one "true" one but looks like all the others is shooting itself in the foot. If you're small and radically different, you can claim that all the world's ills are because your rivals, who are large and influential, are not like you. It's a wonderful advantage to be small, inconsequential, and obscure in the "one true religion"-claiming business.

So I'd shuffle off to the library whenever the threat of birthday cupcakes loomed or a Christmas-themed song was to be sung. A lot of people express sympathy for a child having to miss such fun events, but it's interesting how much I *didn't* miss them. I have no recollection of feeling deprived or being resentful about it. Sure, I didn't enjoy having to make such a public and solitary stand as such a young child, but the objective fact of the situation I had no qualms about. I think it just goes to show how malleable children are. Before the teenage years, they will wholeheartedly believe in and suffer any indignity for what their parents impart to them.

I had a normal number of friends in school; my first cousin was in my second-grade class, so that provided some support. In third grade I was involved in an underground fight club ring, for which we were constantly in danger of being discovered and punished. The penalty would've been a paddling, believe it or not, which is proof that corporal punishment was still alive and well in rural Tennessee in the mid- to late-nineties.

To be honest, the main handicap a Witness kid suffers socially isn't having to explain strange beliefs to teachers and classmates but being prohibited from having any unnecessary contact with other students outside school hours. I think this is a relatively unknown point to non-Witnesses: people, even children, outside the organization are termed worldly and therefore "bad association." No JW can grow up without having 1 Corinthians 15:33 drilled into his head. This was our watchword, this was our creed:

spend only the minimal amount of time necessary with non-Witnesses. You can imagine that there are probably any number of scriptural passages that can be pressed into service for this mindset, despite it in a larger sense running clearly contrary to the spirit of the Gospel and the express example of Christ. (I won't go into them, though; playing Scripture hockey with a Witness is futile most of the time.)

I assure you that we took this counsel very seriously. My father had a workmate of many years, the sort of solid, sturdy fellow you'd trust with your life, and I can recall Dad explaining to us how he was always vigilant to rebuff any attempt by this man to seek a deeper friendship or to involve our families more closely in any way. But if you'd seen these two men work together—the catchphrases and jokes, the familiar exclamations, the understated but deeply intuited camaraderie—you would judge it a great tragedy that this brotherhood was nipped so cruelly in the bud.

When classmates suggested play dates, I knew better than to even ask my parents. I don't believe I once went over to a school friend's house or had one over at mine. Add to this wall of separation another blow to socialization: no extracurricular clubs, activities, or sports. Predictably the reasoning is the same: these require unnecessary exposure to potential contaminants. I grant that parents have a right to control their child's associations, of course. But this was a categorical block for which no exceptions were allowed, not even after proper vetting.

Of all the challenges of growing up as a Witness, these stand out as the most crippling. You can't even begin to conceive of yourself as any part of a community (except the JW community) when these sorts of practical and mental barriers are erected around you. Kids learn so many intangible skills through things like sports and band and clubs. Your life takes on a much more utilitarian hue when school, which is such a major portion of a kid's life, is reduced to the bare minimum experience: just some marks on a report card. Alienation is a huge problem in America today, but I can tell you, for Jehovah's Witnesses, it's baked into the cake from a young age.

All this has a very important purpose: to push Witnesses ever deeper into the arms of their local congregation and the organization generally. Group identities are usually formed most strongly in opposition to other identities. The Witnesses have learned well the lesson of all totalizing ideologies: there can be no competing loyalties. Though the main loyalty to be broken down is the family (and I'll get to how they do that later in the story), other ancillary identities can't be ignored either, if total control is the goal. You're not part of a friend group; you're not an active member of your school; you don't get involved in your community—you don't participate in any of these things, apart from how and when Watchtower tells you to. Watchtower is a jealous god and will suffer no strange gods before it.

Because of this, I didn't feel any real connection to my world growing up. While video games and cell phones make this problem common among non-JWs today as well, that's more of a natural consequence than an artificially enforced situation like this was. Nationality is also not allowed. You are literally not part of the world (John 17:14), meaning I didn't experience the sublime and healthy sentiment of patriotism until I was grown and had left the religion.

To be deprived of patriotism is to live a life with a great hole in it. Many, especially in the modern cynical West, may not put much stock in this, but to gaze at the unfurled flag, or at a beautiful, emblematic landscape, and to feel the onrushing weight of the lives lived and lost, the heroism, the battles fought, and the sometimes tragic humanity with which our people baptized these places truly must be counted as one of the greatest joys of life. I can testify that this experience is not open to a Witness. As I said, no overlapping identities are allowed. Sure, a Witness would understand, as a United States citizen, that he is, by virtue of that fact, "an American," but nothing more would be allowed—nothing that could introduce any dissonance or potential conflict of loyalty. He is a "worshipper of Jehovah," full stop. His friends, his family, and his entire self-conception must be contained within this principle.

One of the amazing things about Catholicism, as I would one day discover, is that it doesn't do that. It's a total ideology and worldview in a certain sense, and yet it somehow assimilates other concepts and identities instead of destroying them. I can think of no other international movement which is simultaneously so local and so particular. Everything under the sun seems comfortable taking its proper place within Catholicism. Local ties, customs, families, even nation states all seem to settle into whatever nook of the larger whole they're fitted for and to flourish there. In fact, Catholicism's notorious concern for the family is telling proof that it's not totalitarian in the negative sense of that term. Totalizing ideologies can brook no competitors, and the greatest competitor to all other identities is the family. To promote family ties, to strengthen this primordial institution's inviolability, is counterproductive if you're aiming at total control. Only an identity that's supremely self-confident and powerfully all-inclusive could do that.

And so that's exactly what the Watchtower *doesn't* do. The JWs give lip service to the family, as all conservative Christian groups must, but in the last analysis, their policies and ethos are destructive to the family through the shunning rule, or what they call "disfellowshipping." When you're disfellowshipped, you're expelled from God's organization and are liable to total destruction if the Apocalypse comes. The temporal penalties are almost as bad, though: no Witness (except for a close relative you live in the same house with or someone you have an indispensable business relationship with) is allowed to eat with you, talk with you—even say a greeting to you. Once again, there's scripture for it (1 Corinthians 5:4–5, 11; 2 John 1:10; 2 Thessalonians 3:14).

Just consider for a moment what that means: the most sacred relationships on earth—father and son, mother and daughter, brother and sister—can be forcefully torn asunder by Watchtower. In what unseen ways does this possibility poison these relations from the start? When a new Witness mother gazes down at her newborn baby, does it enter her mind that, her intense affection for this new life notwithstanding, there could come a day when she'll have to pretend like it doesn't exist? I don't think my mother let herself think such a thing. I think my father did, though. I suspect he owned up to it, faced it squarely, and sounded it down deep into his bones. For that's the only way, when you live authentically in the midst of brutality, to keep your sanity.

I don't think there's any way, if you really get the implications of disfellowshipping, for it not to change your attitude toward your own children, or toward any other human being. They are all on probation. However, as I've intimated, if it was having this effect on my father, I couldn't tell it. I have no complaints with the way he lived out fatherhood. One mismatch we had, though, was that I was so academically inclined. Dad would always assure me that he didn't care how I did in school, as long as I passed. What was more important to him, he'd say, was that I remain a servant of Jehovah. That was the one thing he wanted for me.

Chapter 2

Life Along the Watchtower

At age eight, I was definitely "a servant of Jehovah." I knew my dad was proud of me. I was now giving talks of increasing complexity. I prepared presentations and spoke from the heart when we were "out in service," as Witnesses call their door-to-door proselytizing. That's the activity they are primarily known for. Going out in service is a uniquely Witness life experience. Maybe you'd be surprised to know that the Witnesses have carved up every square inch of the globe into "territories" that are kept on file at each local Kingdom Hall. The individual Witness can check out a territory and "work" it, which means talking to (or at least attempting to talk to) every householder in it. It's a monumental task, but Witnesses are very systematic about it. They keep little sheets sent by Watchtower on which to record the street, house number, and the nature of the interaction.

It's most people's worst nightmare—a combination of public speaking and cold-call salesmanship—but when you're thrust into it from an early age, you really do get used to it. I've no doubt it made me a better public speaker. The classic image is of two suited men with briefcases or two skirted women walking along a quaint neighborhood street taking turns at each house. Most of the territory in rural Tennessee, though, was much more spread out and accessible only by car. We'd get out of the vehicle with a companion, book bag and *Watchtower* magazine in hand. Once we ascertained that the barking guard dogs were sufficiently detained, we'd knock or ring the doorbell, and if someone answered, we'd introduce ourselves and then lead with a question. *Have you ever lost someone you cared about? Have you ever wondered if there will be an end to war? Are you worried about pollution and the future of our planet?* We intentionally asked questions that were that broad and general because we needed topics that anyone could have an opinion about. The next step was to say, "Did you know that the Bible says *x* about that topic?" and then flip open to a Scripture and read it to them. Next, "This month's issue of *The Watchtower* (or *Awake*) looks at how *y* event fulfills Bible prophecy. I'd be glad to leave it with you if you'd be interested in reading it!" If they accepted, we would then say: "And maybe next week I'll come back and see what you thought about it?"

If we were able to place magazines like that, we'd mark that home down for a "return visit" and come back the next week (or when the next issues came out) and repeat the whole process. I never really followed up on what householders thought about the previously placed magazines—seems like most people didn't actually read them, so that question could get awkward. It was taken as a good enough sign for someone merely to accept the magazines, and this little magazine delivery service could continue for months, sometimes years. We were also supposed to suggest a donation be given by the householder, but this was often neglected as well because of the potential awkwardness.

What's the endgame of all this? Conversion, but keep in mind, over the course of eighteen years of preaching experience, for at least six hours every month on average, I only saw the full process play out one, maybe two times that I can recall. Generally you leave magazines with a "call" (someone who has taken the magazines) for several months, and then when you feel the time is right, you ask him if he'd like a free in-home Bible study. The Bible is somewhat secondary to that process, though, because the main thing that's being studied is a heavier brochure or small book which contains references to the Scriptures. Bible study sessions can be thirty minutes to an hour, and the process usually goes through two books of increasing difficulty. These books are re-written every few years.

After completing what's normally a two-book study course, the "study," as he's called, will normally be ready to be examined for baptism. There used to be an exhaustive list of questions that the initiate had to study and for which he had to memorize Scripture references and answers. He's questioned multiple times by various elders, and, if he provides satisfactory answers and evidences a heartfelt desire, he will be cleared for "dedication and baptism."

Baptism is what makes one liable for shunning, so it's a big step. They don't dwell on this fact during the preparation process, but they won't deny it either. I don't remember giving it a second thought because the idea of leaving or committing a serious sin was too unthinkable. But anyway, I can only recall one or two studies (i.e., potential converts) completing the process. The thing was—forgive my bluntness—it was never some upstanding person of means or a "respectable" family—people who converted were usually somewhat down and out, or in precarious circumstances, or just seemed a bit "off."

For instance, one of my dad's studies that I believe made it all the way through baptism was the type of middle-aged man to whom you might give a ride to the Greyhound bus station and never hear from again. Or it was a single mom with multiple jobs and kids who became a devoted Witness in the wake of her abandonment. If you're down and out or in need of an intense social support system, the "love-bombing" that the Witnesses (and most high-control groups) do can seem like an oasis. How else can you make dozens of new friends all at once that would give you the shirts off their backs? But people that already have a lot going for them—money, friends, stable families, social prestige—these types of people rarely, if ever, become Witnesses anymore.

Whether that was always the case, I can't say. I assume at some point it wasn't because any organization would need people of means to support it initially to get it off the ground. In my own family, it seems to have been a mixed bag. On my father's side, I'm a fifth-generation Witness, believe it or not, meaning my great-great grandfather was the first to convert and die a Witness. My grandfather remembered painting the first Kingdom Hall in Nashville, and we're connected to a lot of the oldest Witness families. One of my great-grandmothers on that side of the family was at the much-touted International Convention at Yankee Stadium in New York City in 1950. From family stories and my own research, it seems like my paternal great-great grandfather wasn't very ambitious, and he never really settled on a profession. It doesn't appear he ever owned property, even though his father was pretty successful and owned a farm. It's not hard to imagine such a man being attracted to a purer, more exclusive sect that turned its back on worldly success.

The roots on my mother's side aren't as deep. Her parents converted (I think) at the same time that my grandmother's mother and sisters all did. My grandfather on that side had a rough upbringing (his mother died when he was young, and his father had health issues), but he did start his own concrete pouring business that's still in operation. My guess is that he was disgusted with this hypocritical world and that the Witnesses won him over by proving that they were no part of it. I couldn't tell you what motivates my grandmother other than that she seems to believe devoutly and sincerely everything Watchtower teaches.

Regardless, the families you'll find today are mostly people who were raised in it or converted a long time ago, at least in the developed Western countries. What's fortunate for the Witnesses is that there's plenty of Scriptural cover for this—the path is narrow and few are those finding it (Matthew 7:13–14); only the meek and simple will inherit the Kingdom (Matthew 5:5; 18:3), etc. Daddy always made much of how rich people never converted, frequently quoting Christ to that effect (Matthew 19:23).

Dovetailing with that is the style of JW material. Their website is written at a surprisingly basic reading level, and the presenters on JW Broadcasting speak as if they're presenting children's media. Now, I'm not saying that every church brochure or sermon needs to be the *Summa Theologica*, but JW content is almost disturbingly simplistic, as if they're nefariously talking down to their audience. We're all familiar with the horror movie trope of the sadistic clinical authority that calmly tells you in a monotone that he's going to lobotomize you or something—that's the vibe that their videos give off. It's robotic and creepy. The subtext moving throughout all their videos is, "We know you're just overjoyed to learn from us what God wants of you. We're sure you would never doubt what we're telling you, now would you?"

In later years I asked Dad why Witness literature was written as if for children, and he responded by quoting Scripture to the effect that "the truth" (that's what Witnesses call their religion in casual conversation) is not for the wise and haughty but for the unlettered and ordinary (Matthew 11:25).

Going out for two to three hours a week peddling this stuff was my life from before I can remember. As you get older, you become deathly afraid of running into one of your classmates during this activity. Sure, they all know you're a Witness, but to be exposed doing this strange thing and to have to give the whole sales pitch to them is very embarrassing, even if you're a serious youngster like I was. It happened to me a few times.

Besides two to three hours of door-to-door work, there were other activities throughout the week: a one-hour "book study" at another Witness family's home, an hour-and-a-half skills and information training at the Kingdom Hall, and a two-hour Public Talk and Watchtower Study. Oh, and not to mention family study night, which was probably forty-five minutes. It wasn't enforced, but good Witnesses like my dad invariably observed it. That's over eight hours of meetings and activities per week. And of course preparation time is all in addition to that. You were also supposed to be reading both the Bible and the newly issued books and magazines in your spare time.

Now, some of this has been reduced in recent years (book study was folded into one of the other meetings), and I'm certainly not someone who thinks religion in general should be *less* a part of most people's lives, but I think anyone would admit that that's a full schedule. Something I've heard is that high-control groups routinely try to fill their members' schedules as one of their tools of control. I'm not sure exactly what that does psychologically, but from my experience it seems like it does help keep people invested. You're much less likely to admit you were mistaken and up and leave an organization if you never have time to stop and think about it, or you've invested so much time and energy into it that you can't face the possibility that it might've been a waste.

That's something, as a convert, that's always fascinated me. The majority of people, it seems, don't change their beliefs drastically during their lifetimes. What confluence of factors can dispose a person to admit he was wrong about something as deeply personal as religion? The Witnesses don't leave much to chance with that. Indeed, along with all I've mentioned, there's an absolute prohibition on reading, not just anti-Witness literature, but any religious material not created by Watchtower. Try this out next time the Witnesses come to your door: tell them you'll take and read their magazines if they'll promise to do the same with something from your religious belief system, if you have one. I guarantee you they will decline the offer—they're not allowed to do otherwise. As a young minister this happened to me once with some Mormons, and when I came back to the car with a *Book of Mormon* in hand, I was told, "We don't do that."

What did I think about being told that? I can't remember if that was the beginning of my doubts, but if it wasn't, it should have been. Sadly, I think the book ban generally keeps more people *in* the Witnesses than it chases away, because it's so total. I remember almost superstitiously not wanting to peer into any non-JW religious book, and I was assured that all churches besides Kingdom Halls were the haunts of demons. It wasn't even safe to enter one for a club or a charity. To this day even going into a church basement is a little uncanny for me.

If someone tries to "argue" with you at the door (which is the term Witnesses use for anyone that tries to bring their own religious views into the discussion), that person is labeled a "goat-like one," their house is marked, and only elders or very spiritually mature ones may call there again, and only to see if they've softened. I've gone back and forth as to why Witnesses are so allergic to any kind of religious discussion on equal grounds. What does leadership not have confidence in: the rank and file's ability to defend their beliefs unless there's zero pushback, or the beliefs themselves? Sure, religious debate isn't everyone's thing; it can be notoriously heated and emotional. But if you're going around trying to convert people, what do you expect?

My theory is that they've simply made a cold calculation: the number of Witnesses they'd lose from having their beliefs potentially discredited exceeds, in their estimation, the number that will get suspicious of this sheltered mentality and go on to challenge their beliefs themselves. In fact, let me tell you why most people, in my experience, leave. It has nothing to do with "facts and logic," good arguments, or being challenged. In most cases, it's just hurt feelings and anger over hypocrisy.

A family close to ours illustrated this. The father had a factory job, and that job required him to work one Sunday a month. Because of his status as a ministerial servant (one step below an elder), this was a big problem. In the Witness world, there's this important concept of "exemplary conduct." To hold a position such as ministerial servant, you've got to exhibit exemplary conduct; otherwise, people will talk and scandal will arise.

The elders approached him one day and explained to him that he would need to either step down from his position, or he would be removed. One of these elders had a well-paying job that allowed him flexibility in his schedule, a job that was made possible by his post-secondary education. The irony was lost on the elder.

He and his family then performed what ex-Witnesses call a "slow fade," which basically means a gradual withdrawal from all aspects of JW life. The elders will attempt to make "shepherding calls" on inactive Witnesses, but they won't beat your door down and drag you before a tribunal if you avoid them, and they won't disfellowship you *in absentia* in most cases. The line taken with those who drift away and take no public action against their former faith is gentler than that taken with those whose rebellion is explicit. The Witnesses are much more agreeable to their former members being stuck in a kind of belief system limbo than they are to people who find a positive expression of new beliefs afterward. In this I must admit they are not unique among religions; the Catholic Church prefers lapsed

Catholics to apostate ones, though there are no social threats backing up this preference.

And interestingly, those who drift into inactivity through discouragement are generally not rebels and so remain in part psychologically captive to the belief system. This is what's going on when an active Witness says about one of these individuals, "I don't know why he left; he knows it's the truth." To a certain extent, he's right: inactive Witnesses that don't make a clear and principled break with the organization take years to decolonize their minds of Witness beliefs. An inactive relative of mine recently told me, in effect: "It's not that I'm rejecting what I was taught; it's that I think the earthly part of the organization is hypocritical and defective."

To me that's the most lamentable of all attitudes. It's also an absurdity. The beliefs a former Witness was taught do not permit him to believe a thing like "the earthly part is defective." There are many ex-Witnesses, in my experience, who carry baggage with them from their former mindset for years afterward. It could be that they still don't celebrate Christmas or birthdays, or maybe they hold onto their cynicism regarding other religions or society as a whole. If they're faced with a life-threatening medical situation involving blood loss, perhaps they're unexpectedly wracked with guilt over taking a blood transfusion. I want to ask such people: what are you holding on to? You already stand condemned by Watchtower. By not practicing and preaching, you've already rejected the most crucial elements of the whole system! There's a wide, beautiful world of freedom on the other side— the freedom to experience a full life, the freedom to insert yourself into the great stream of human existence. Cleanse your mind and go read about philosophy, religion, and science. Go join a church or volunteer for a charity. Discover your roots. You're now free to be a part of your community. The whole of life is now open to you.

A very different vista was opening up for me, though, at the age of about 8 or 9. I was getting noticed in our tiny congregation as a "young one" with quite a promising future. I continued to give my talks and speak from the heart out in field service, and midway through my third-grade year, my parents decided to move to a slightly larger town west of Nashville. Our only connection to the place was that my dad had worked in the mobile home business there for several years. I think my mother was also getting tired of her roots and was wanting to create some distance again. Some of my first cousins had moved a few hours away to Putnam County the previous year, so there was less keeping us where we were. After we moved, we commuted back to my elementary school, staying overnight with my grandparents part of the time. It's strange to think back on various impressions from this patchwork of childhood memories, with their hazy, dreamlike quality. Seemingly insignificant things stick with you: a green, leafy blur, hurtling along a two-lane highway at dusk through the remote wilderness, for example. It's slightly alarming how little else I remember from this or many other periods of life: just strong impressions of various landscapes or places.

We moved into a duplex not far from downtown. The plan, again, was for Daddy to build us another house. This was one of my favorite places that we lived. It was an older part of town that felt like an actual neighborhood—the streets were more regular, and the houses were closer together. We made acquaintances with the next-door neighbors, who had two boys named Josh and Scooby, young daredevils. We could walk down the street to the elementary school and play on the playground equipment there.

Possibly the greatest consequence of moving where we did was meeting the closest friend I've had, Levi. I remember our mothers introducing us in the Kingdom Hall parking lot. I was suspicious at first, but I don't know why—maybe I thought his name was strange. The parallel journeys we were to take in life can only be chalked up to God's gratuitous providential care.

We played video games sometimes, but our imaginative world was still rich. Building on a custom mythology inspired by cardboard cut-outs in a store that my cousins and I encountered, we imagined the supernatural Dairy Man (a mutation, somehow, of a cut-out of the Maytag man we'd seen there) and his ghostly cronies coming after us: the Punching Man, the Green Man, and their supporting spooks the Woman in White, the Paradox Man, and the Dead Boy (all taken loosely from horror television shows like *Are You Afraid of the Dark?*). The excitement we had narrowly escaping from their clutches can't be overstated. Part of the magic of childhood is just this thrill in imagining danger and adventure. It's why I'm convinced that all attempts to sanitize childhood from exposure to such things, whether that be the contemporary culture's purging of death and violence from all children's media, or the fundamentalist attempts to whitewash Halloween, are misguided. Children used to be exposed to Grimm's fairy tales and to a whole lore of spooky traditional stories on which they no doubt meditated apprehensively after dark. Now all they'll get is googly-eyed anthropomorphic animals lecturing them about being nice to people.

Daddy finished that third house south of town. There was more grass and some adjacent woods I could roam around in, but I don't generally remember the house positively: to me, the area seemed kind of desolate. There was a trailer park backing up to it that I was not supposed to go in, but which seemed to have a more lively neighborhood scene. Levi grew up in the same house his entire childhood, so that provided some continuity for our adventures. His house was more in-town but somehow still surrounded by a dense wood that is shrouded in mystical memory for me. There's something about living in one place through multiple stages of life that creates a rich, multi-layered texture to the experience and memory of the place. I can think back on that house and property and feel the many episodes it was host to: young boys keen on harrowing adventures; teenagers on the edge of the night; and young adults with a maturing and mellowing sense of their place in the world. There are enchanted realms, dangerous and rebellious escapades, and sober reflections all held in vivid stasis on that piece of property, like a living museum for anyone who was privileged enough to be there. It almost seems too much that those times are over, that the true nature of that place will be locked away from all future inhabitants once we're gone. How many such places there must be that we all move through every day, with no knowledge of their true meaning! It must be that Heaven is partly the proper appreciation of these things universally: the opening of our eyes to the invisible treasures that have always surrounded us.

In the new house in the big field (the owners after us would turn it into a small horse farm), I entered middle school. The elementary school where I had attended the fourth and fifth grades was one of those wholesome, newer suburban schools. Sixth grade at the middle school was in a dilapidated old building near downtown that seemed designed to introduce innocent youths to the period class schedule, no recess, and the gutter talk of adolescence. I learned about many novel concepts from a streetwise new companion. I had to go home that night and ask my dad about the various euphemisms I'd learned.

Daddy told me such things were wrong and that I should stop associating with those boys. I decided I'd do one better: I'd convert them. I'm not sure how much effect I had over that year, but at one point I did get the worst offender ostracized from the group. Those three years of middle school were a strange time in my development, however, that would culminate in one of the biggest mistakes of my young life.

I think it began as a result of my mingled disgust, fascination, and fear of the very teenage world opening up before me. In the beginning I variously dabbled in it and reacted against it. I was a conscientious boy, and so I consulted my father frequently about what I was seeing and hearing. It soothed my conscience. What was in the world did not match the morality of my JW upbringing. I tried to deal with this cognitive dissonance by confessing my sins to my dad many evenings. I don't think it was concerning to him that I was possibly doing this in an obsessive or compulsive way. I really think he was just glad to keep these channels of communication open and to be able to shape my worldview as it was being assaulted by the outside world. Maybe my father encouraged me to more totally reject these forces, or maybe the fortress mentality I was adopting came to me completely naturally. Either way, I think he judged that whatever was going on in me was preferable to the typical teenage alternative. But that would come in time.

During sixth grade I maintained my public profile, seeking to lead the fallen to my way of thinking, almost like a "hip" square. But as I progressed to seventh grade, my rejection of the world drove me into a sort of escapist posture. For leisure, this looked like more video games and comic books, and eventually online websites and forums for these things. After all, if a boy is not allowed to play sports or get involved in extracurricular activities, what else is he going to do? I knew enough not to be up front or public about these nerdy pastimes, but it certainly began to affect my social standing. My parents weren't thrilled about all this, but what was the alternative? I think maybe Dad thought I'd just play outside all day like he did as a kid, which I did some, but trees and rocks aren't as thrilling when you've got interactive digital reality waiting for you inside.

Should I have been allowed to play video games? In a vacuum, I think video games are like any form of media: sometimes fulfilling and edifying and sometimes degrading and worthless. I have fond memories of many of them, such as *The Legend of Zelda*: mostly ones that tell a story or try to evoke a sense of wonder. In that sense many of them are no different than a good book or movie, acting as a mirror to life. The problem, I think, even with the "good" ones, is that kids aren't really equipped to use them correctly: their still-developing brains don't need to have addictive, all-encompassing new realities created for them out of whole cloth. They need to be deriving that sense of wonder and excitement from the world they actually live in.

I think video game immersion can alienate children from a full-throated experience of the real world. Instead of learning to shoot squirrels with an air rifle, they learn to shoot virtual AR-15s with their thumbs. Instead of catching a glimpse of a real wild animal, they're busy waiting in virtual grass for a Pokémon. Instead of learning about courtship and romance by talking to a real girl, their avatar online is talking up a virtual love interest. It seems counterintuitive, but I think video games are best left as a casual diversion for adults (though we'll see if I've changed my tune when my son comes of age). Again, it's not that I don't have fond memories of some of them, or that their effect on my imagination was always negative—some of them may have risen to the level of art. It's just that, on the whole, my obsessive, underdeveloped young brain was probably stunted in some way by its reliance on them.

And it's many times worse for boys today: many of the games are not about a story or characters, but are purely online multiplayer diversions. Young men spend hours honing their skills on these pointless games. Maybe it's alright to hang out on Friday night with your buddies and play a shooter together, but this endless online content with strangers is a waste of time: no camaraderie with real people (besides their disembodied voices) is built, no dramatic storylines with the potential to enrich or teach are experienced, and no physical prowess is developed (as would be with sports). Just endless rounds of thumb twitching and progress that evaporates when a new game comes out.

Apart from games, my retreat from the world involved an increasing seriousness about religion. In addition to my detailed and embarrassing confessions to my dad, I began trying in earnest to complete the great schedule of activities Watchtower holds out for its followers. If you'll recall, the point is not to complete all the tasks—this would be quite impossible. The point is to keep even the most obsessive Witness perpetually busy. No matter what your level of dedication, there's always more to do.

But nobody told me that. I set out to seriously fulfill all my religious obligations. This meant not only field service, all three meetings, family study, and preparation for all those meetings, but also a program of personal study: private study of Watchtower publications and a personal program of Bible reading. It got to the point where I was upstairs in the study reading and marking up magazines from the time I got home from school to the time I was called down for supper, and then some. And I was perpetually getting behind: not getting through both meeting prep and personal study on a Wednesday, for example, and having to double up my load on days off. It kind of felt like I was running the *Supersize Me*[1] experiment (that is, taking the company at their word and swallowing the entire Watchtower program as advertised) and being crushed under the weight of it.

I've always been a little obsessive about consistency. It's a defect and a virtue: if I'm going to do or believe something, I'm going to do it fully and completely, and I'm going to believe it wholeheartedly or not at all. The code of "logic" I feel compelled to live by demands it. That seems to be a feature of highly idealistic people. Most people don't seem as concerned about chasing down and rooting out inconsistencies in their beliefs, and in some ways I envy them. Perhaps there's a sort of "midwit" hubris about believing it's even possible to live a logically airtight and consistent life. How could anyone's limited mind objectively grasp the totality and complexity of it all? And what larger contradictions are uncovered by the ruthless pursuit of logical purity? Regardless of the answers to these questions, such has ever been my way of life.

I still had my friends at the Kingdom Hall, Levi and Jeremy, and starting in eighth grade, my first cousin, who had been living in Putnam County and had moved now to our town. We four, along with an older JW guy named Mike, formed the nucleus of the running group that would support my later teenage rebellion.

But for now I was doggedly pursuing Witness purity. I was studying more, commenting more at meetings, and avoiding bad influences more completely. Leadership was seeing a lot of potential in me. Someone floated the idea: what prevents this boy from getting baptized? Baptism is usually not until age fifteen or sixteen, but I was progressing so rapidly that it seemed unnecessary to wait.

Waiting until at least age fifteen for baptism as a JW makes sense on several levels. First, it's generally tough for people younger than that to pass the required battery of questions. Second, most teens have settled into whatever pattern of obedience or rebellion they're going to pursue by that point. A generally well-balanced, average Witness at this age will usually be able to accept the idea of being a Witness for the rest of his life and then stick to that commitment. On the other hand, if the Witness was going to

---

1. Spurlock, *Super Size Me*.

be a chronic problem child or simply wasn't the type who could handle being policed and questioned constantly, that would probably be apparent by age fifteen, and all involved could agree he should wait to be baptized. So it's really a natural break point: late enough in life that everyone can see where the person is headed, but early enough to ensnare the ones that were less likely to stray anyway. It's in no one's interest to baptize someone who is just going to get shunned in a couple years, but the threat of shunning is a nice safeguard for those that already seem stable.

What was the calculus with me? I was only eleven years old, not even a teenager. I was still quite obedient and deferent to my parents and was easily influenced by them and other adults in authority. Their thought was probably that baptism is good, and if he's ready, why delay?

Witnesses openly acknowledge that the fear of being shunned is a positive side effect of their system—it'll keep you on track when your resolve wavers. That's somewhat excusable when you're talking about a fifteen-year-old, who, like I said, has probably revealed his true colors by that point. Even though he's still a minor, you could make a better argument that he knows what he's getting himself into. Not so with an eleven-year-old. Perhaps they thought it worth the gamble, though: that maybe "making it official" and bringing the threat of shunning over me would lock my Witness power-level in place, so to speak. Maybe it would keep me from going off the rails in the first place. I don't know if any considerations like these entered the calculations, but I almost don't see how they couldn't have. If you ask a Witness on the street about shunning, you'll be hard-pressed to get any information out of him. But each one understands the practice clearly, make no mistake.

My obsessive-compulsive turn, then, had led me to early-onset baptism. Describing it in such negative terms may strike you as the typical convert animosity towards one's former beliefs. I'd certainly be lying if I said I wasn't hostile to the JW faith and organization, but I assure you, my spiritual state during this time of intense JW service was not healthy. I was wracked with guilt over my daily sins, most nights having to confess anew to my father. I was bogged down in hours of personal study with a never-ending backlog of material to get through, and I increasingly desired alienation from the larger society, childishly retreating into a comfortable imaginative world. Obsessive and compulsive are the only words for it, though I don't think anyone was truly aware of how insular I'd become. I'm sure a Witness could argue it wasn't the goal of their religion and that many serious members are healthy and well-adjusted, and I'm sure there's an army of former Catholics who'd like to tell me how the practice of my current religion did something similar to them. But I want to maintain, in the face of all that, that the JW faith *is* what caused my pitiful psychological state.

It shouldn't be that hard to see why: I described of course the withering barrage of tasks that any JW should at least feel some obligation to undertake, though, humanly speaking, few could finish them all. My honest sense is that the JW faith is more like a "Communist Party of God" than it is like other Christian denominations. People become communists (or used to; you don't hear about it much anymore) because they have a deep sense of justice and, having washed their hands of all that this bourgeois world is, are ready to work and even die for a future utopia. I put to you that a very similar motivation drives many Witnesses. This is a common refrain: "I grew up around the churches of Christendom" (the Witness term for any non-JW Christian group). "Mostly just hypocrites, just in it for the power and the money. That's why you see them get tangled up in this old system's wars and corruption. Catholics" (or insert name of religious group here) "will wave the flag and go to war and kill one another. But Jehovah's organization is different. We're politically neutral, so we'll never be killing one another in man's wars. We remain without spot from the world."

A major part of the motivation I've observed is akin to the utopianism you see in leftist philosophies: this world and its institutions are incurably corrupt: we withdraw from them and seek their overthrow. With communists that's some kind of violent upheaval; with Witnesses it's neutrality now and a violent removal by God later. Similarly, the communist diligently devotes his life now to rallying and organizing and pamphleteering to hasten the day of the revolution while the Witness attends meetings and shares his faith and distributes literature all with a view toward fulfilling the Bible prophecy that must be fulfilled before the day of Armageddon. It's all part of an ineluctable process in both systems, yet in both the utmost urgency is still demanded of the individual adherent.

So I don't think it's any wonder I was becoming neurotic. Deriving your meaning in life from a schedule of tasks to be completed, regardless of whether those tasks are ordered to a political-revolutionary end or a political-spiritual one, will always leave one wanting.

My experience is that true religion is much more about *acceptance* and *being* than striving and doing (striving and doing have a role, for sure, but that role is secondary). But Witness theology cuts off acceptance at the knees and seriously hinders this maturation process in its members. It does this primarily by removing the concept of God's passive will.

The idea in most Christian theology is that, because God is both omnipotent and all good, the explanation for evil is that God only passively wills it. This is opposed to his active will, which would include his creation of the world, or some miraculous action he accomplishes in a person's life. If God didn't will the evil things that occur at least in some way, they couldn't exist, and so the passive will amounts to a sort of divine toleration. In the case of evil, this toleration only occurs because it is necessary for a greater good; namely, the existence of love and the free choice love requires.

The Witnesses have a different theory. The central axiom of their theology is sovereignty, or who reigns. According to them, the original question posed in the garden of Eden was whether man had the right or ability to rule himself. Satan convinced man that he could rule himself independently of God. The sordid tale of human history is the result. And that tale, in their telling, is one of manmade governments failing again and again to establish just rule. The Devil's bargain at Eden, then, was that God allowed man to go his own way, so to speak—meaning that God largely abandoned man to his fate and relinquished control of human history. Sure, God still intervenes on occasion to accomplish some limited goal (such as the Great Flood, the Incarnation, the establishment of the Watchtower organization, or even the favorable deals Witnesses sometimes get on future Kingdom Hall sites), but besides these instances of the active will, humans are basically adrift in the universe. When bad things happen, it's just the random reverberations emanating from original sin. There's no rhyme or reason or greater good ultimately in view.

I'm sure there's a rogue's gallery of atheists howling, "Greater good? What monster would allow one one-hundredth of the Holocaust to occur for some hypothetical 'greater good'?" I want to focus, though, on how the rejection of this belief affects the Witnesses. Their system requires them to reject an ordering providence in daily life because the whole point of history, according to them, is to prove that man's governments inevitably result in death, suffering, and the destruction of the natural world. This has two practical effects on Witness life and piety. One is that it grounds eschatologically their complete non-involvement in political affairs and government. Two, it gives them another distinctive that helps in their polemics. In much of popular Christianity, when someone dies, well-wishers will try to console the bereaved by assuring them that "God just needed another angel," or "God took your loved one because he wanted to be with him." While these commonplaces are technically problematic, as I'll admit, they do imply a belief in an omniscient providence that ultimately is providing for our good. The Witness scoffs at these in much the same way the nonbeliever does. "Your God kills and takes people? Your God is responsible for all this? What a monster!"

The unintended consequence of this "point scored" against traditional Christianity, though, is that the world becomes a much more dangerous and capricious place. God intervenes at times of course (usually to assist in some Witness endeavor or project), but otherwise, nothing stands between the Witness and Satan's chaotic, death-dealing world. "The world is in the power of the wicked one" (1 John 5:19), and as far as Witnesses are concerned, that means everything God doesn't intentionally accomplish is the work of the Devil.

This belief system doesn't do a lot to inspire confidence in the ultimate goodness of the course of events, whether that be in the wide sweep of history or in one's daily life. That's really much of the point of religion, though: a sense of meaning and direction in the face of seemingly meaningless suffering and what can feel like a purposeless existence. My intense religiosity, therefore, did not include a heightened sense of God's protecting care or a confidence in his ways. It was simply, do more for Jehovah and his organization.

It's always perilous criticizing spiritualities because it can cut both ways. There is no shortage of Catholics who live vapid, small-minded, materialistic lives, to say nothing of those actively perpetrating evil and harm. But Catholicism shouldn't be judged by the conduct of the many who don't take it seriously. There are people of every tribe, tongue, and nation and from every age, who have taken her at her word—and the results are undeniable. These are the saints, and if you want to see what Catholicism will do for your life if you actually practice it, look no further than these.

The Witnesses, like most Protestants, have no "saints." The very concept is idolatrous to them. So a one-to-one comparison isn't possible. One thing that illustrates the differences is that Witnesses don't do humanitarian work for non-Witnesses. They say they don't need to provide for the body of their fellow man because they give him something far more important: truth for his soul. They also point to the intense "love among the brothers" as evidence of being Christ's true followers (John 13:35). It seems quite a blind spot, though, to leave out the rest of suffering mankind when Christ said those who didn't care for these least ones were not his followers (Matthew 25:45).

I don't think you're going to find the type of peaceful, disinterested love from the Witnesses that you'd find from, say, Mother Teresa. If you're not showing signs of converting, you're not really worth their time. Evangelization is important, certainly, but Catholicism understands that *people* are valuable in and of themselves. We worship God, we experience God, in each unique and unrepeatable human, no matter how they relate to our goals, however "theocratic" and praiseworthy these goals might be. Catholicism is broad and confident enough not to need every encounter to be a formal proposition to convert.

I feel safe in asserting that practicing Witness religion as intensely and consistently as my eleven-year-old self did resulted in me becoming a neurotic wreck, and the fact that I am (arguably) not one today, suggests to me that Witness life (and life in any high-control social group) is more like working as a political party activist than it is like what most people would call "religion." I was reaching for the next rank of party membership (baptism). Blame my particular experience of JW religion on my personality or psychology, but my experience in later life proves to me that these tendencies can be healed in large part by healthy spiritual praxis.

Witnesses, as I said, get baptized at regional-level assemblies and conventions. Our congregation was zoned for Memphis for spring and fall assemblies and Alabama for the larger summer convention. The timing of my baptism prep meant I would be baptized at the Assembly Hall of Jehovah's Witnesses in Midtown Memphis, which is a unique location because it's one of the few such facilities owned by Jehovah's Witnesses (usually they just rent gymnasiums and arenas for these larger events). The hall in Memphis is a distinctly urban location, which I appreciated even at a young age. I had always been fascinated by cities—my father's line is from Nashville, as I mentioned, and so visits to Grandma and certain aunts and uncles took place in the big city. That may be the reason for the positive association in my head, but I like to think it's also because I intuited that these were more natural environments than most of the ones I grew up around.

That may sound counterintuitive—I grew up in the country, right? So why would a city be more "natural"? It's because growing up in "the country" these days largely means growing up in the suburbs. You might have a home in the country, to which you retire after work or school, but the places where you live in public—where you shop, work, play, and go to school—are suburban in form for the vast majority of Americans. What I mean by suburban is that they're designed for the car. Having a car is the prerequisite for experiencing these places in the way they were meant to be experienced.

Until we moved into the house I was to live in during high school, I was almost never able to walk to a store or to a friend's house. Every trip to anything required a car. We all imagine that kids grow up in a *Sandlot*-esque environment, organizing impromptu baseball games with the kids down the block. Very few do in reality. Suburban homes provide a premium of private space, but at the cost of convenient public space. This combined with smaller family size means American kids have a lot of their own space but no one to share it with, unless Mommy drives them across town for a playdate. The liberating freedom of just being able to walk over to a friend's house is a freedom most Americans have never known.

Suburbs are the compromise between urban and rural that does justice to neither. You're spread out enough to feel disconnected from your neighbors but not enough to be truly out in nature. And even when you do live out in nature, as we did at that time, you're still living a suburban lifestyle: driving long miles every day to get to work or wherever. Some people may consider this an acceptable price for peaceful evenings on their secluded private porch, but it shouldn't be the norm. It eats up too much countryside and hollows out too much of our cities. We can all drive to Wal-Mart, so we don't need a local corner grocer anymore. I wish I did need one.

The gentleman farmer with the country estate who rides into town to do business used to be something confined to the aristocracy. While unfair, this kept the phenomenon in check: there weren't enough aristocrats around to create anything like the suburban sprawl we see today. But isn't that so much of what's wrong with opulent America? We've democratized so many things that previously only the wealthy had access to, with many unintended consequences. Give everyone a car and a thirty-year mortgage, and pretty soon McMansions and strip malls coat the land. Give everyone cheap, calorically rich food, and obesity skyrockets. Living standards and freedom are important, but some things can't be done by everyone without everyone being made worse off for it. This is "the tragedy of the commons."

My tragedy was just beginning.

Chapter 3

Dedication, Rebellion, and New Gods

That very urban corner of Memphis was where we journeyed to, year after year, for assemblies. The year of my baptism was no different. It was about a two-and-a-half-hour drive. I was nervous but sure of myself: as far as I understood, this was the right thing to do. Jehovah God, as I understood him, wanted me to do this. My parents wanted me to do this. All the older, influential men in the congregation wanted me to do this. The only reason for not doing it? Only that I might want to sin one day? Surely that was a bad reason. Surely the right course was to do what I knew was right, no matter what "could" happen in the future. And so, after walking out on stage in my trunks and t-shirt, and after stepping down into the baptismal pool, I closed my eyes and uttered, "Thank you, Jehovah," as the attendant plunged me beneath the waters.

Witnesses don't believe in sacraments, or what Catholics describe as outward signs or actions that effect what they signify. To a Catholic, baptism actually washes away sin and initiates salvation in a person. For Witnesses, baptism is an outward sign that is superfluously completed *after* some inward act of the will takes place in the believer. Baptism is basically just a "coming out" party as a dedicated Witness, then, and is not to be seen as itself accomplishing anything. Such would be "magical thinking." Yet, transgress this "symbol" after the fact, and be prepared for the swiftest and harshest of consequences. I had little thought of these consequences at the time. But as the weight of my commitments grew, and my psychological state worsened, my subconscious started to look for a way out—regardless of the cost.

People don't change their beliefs when they're content. Every conversion story, therefore, starts with some twinge of discomfort, some irritation or perceived lack. For me this came first of all from the guilt and endless workload my JW perfectionism laid on me. I've mentioned the nightly confessions, the long hours studying, the mounting backlog. You might say, "Wouldn't Witnesses not want people to burn out? I can't believe what you're telling me about the workload. That must've just been your unhealthy perception of it." I would be inclined to agree with you but for the numerous examples in their literature practically castigating Witnesses for holding back their "best" from Jehovah, not giving "whole-souled devotion," or putting worldly and material goods before "spiritual" ones. What job can you quit? How many possessions can you sell? Which associates can you cut off? These are the leading questions week after week. There's no end of doing good, and there's no limit to how much better you might be able to serve. As I explained earlier, though, this kind of "what have you done for me lately?" mentality is necessary for high-control groups. So the only part my neuroticism had in this drama was in taking Watchtower at its word about all this.

The second factor was, as the Watchtower had warned me again and again, my associates. My friends, Levi, Jeremy, Mike, and my cousin Javin. The main difference between them and me was the type of dads we had. I've described my father at length: consistent to a fault, stern but loving. Jeremy's father was basically not around, while Levi's dad and Javin's dad (my uncle) were more distant, gruffer. Levi's parents would eventually leave the religion quietly after several clashes with the elders, while my uncle also went inactive after studying Darwinism. Mike's dad was an elder like mine but cut from a different mold.

No matter how hard mommas try, it's the father who sets the religious tone of the household. Our situations bore this out. As we entered into those fraught teenage years, the drive for independence was taking root. Daddy was intent on me not hurling myself down into the pit via sex, drugs, and alcohol. His plan for this consisted of seemingly tight control of my coming and going. It wasn't a bad strategy. Maybe if not for my friends, it would've worked. But even this chief bulwark that Dad had erected against the onslaught of the world, the flesh, and the devil—my coterie of JW buddies—was a sleeper cell of the enemy, already deep behind friendly lines.

I don't remember the discreet instances that caused the first rumblings of my discontent, but the issue was very clearly that my friends were getting to do things that I was not. We were entering high school. We were getting cars and trucks. A big, wide world was calling us. It was all off-limits to me, though. I was stuck counting my sins each night, and my friends were starting to go to parties, starting to meet girls. If you asked them how all this fit with being a Witness, I don't think they could've answered you. Like most teenagers, developing an airtight system of logic for why their actions were consistent with their beliefs wasn't really a priority. But it was for me.

I think the internet can be a tool for great good or great ill. I am eternally grateful, though, for all the internet authors who have made libraries' worth of information available for free. It was from this well that I began to drink when my frustration with my current belief system came to a head.

Jehovah's Witnesses are old earth creationists, which means they don't believe in Darwinian evolution but do believe the earth could be billions of years old. As I subconsciously set out to jettison my old belief system, my mind went immediately to these Christianity-wide debates. What did I care whether we were saved by faith alone or not or if God was a trinity? Changing those beliefs meant I'd only be scrapping one repressive fundamentalism for another. Besides, my entire training as a Witness had been in why those non-Witness beliefs are false, so to me the only live question was whether the JWs were correct or not. If they could be proven false, in my mind, the whole concept of religion would fall.

Although today I don't have a strong opinion either way on the question of how God created—by theistic evolution or by special creation—at that time in my life, I became thoroughly convinced of the case for evolution, and many of those beliefs have yet to be falsified for me. Whether this is because I haven't revisited the question in recent years, I can't say. These days I am at least open to non-evolutionary Catholic theories of creation. Since converting, though, it's never been an issue on which my faith has stood or fallen. It's always seemed more of a technical question than a doctrinal one.

However, for Witnesses, it certainly is a doctrinal question, and one on which the veracity of the Bible very much stands or falls. They have released several books and brochures over the years dealing with the subject, though I doubt much in them was original research. I set about comparing these creationist sources with the Darwinist websites I found online, most of which seemed squarely aimed at proving the Bible to be a pitifully ignorant Bronze Age fairy tale. Things like Noah's flood, and various chronological aspects of the Genesis account, were special targets. The effect on me was instantaneous. If what they were saying was trustworthy—and why wouldn't it be: science is objective, right?—then believing in a literal reading of the Bible was literally ludicrous!

The transformation in my thinking occurred almost overnight. It was all a lie, then: science explained everything, there probably was no God, and most importantly, I didn't have to listen to the Witnesses because they were wrong too. My mind was abuzz with all the possibilities: a girlfriend, parties, popularity, alcohol—the sky was the limit. If the Witnesses were wrong, then all the religious people were wrong, and the only measure of right or wrong was whether you did physical harm to somebody. No more guilt!

But one dread reality lay buried under all the excitement: the possibility—nay, the inevitability—of my eventual shunning. I had lasted a mere three years as a dedicated Witness, and for the first time it dawned on me what that eleven-year-old's decision would mean for the rest of my life. I weighed my options. I liked the idea of standing up for what I believed and going down in a blaze of glory. But at this stage, that would only bring more repression. If I wanted to live in accord with my newfound libertine beliefs, I would need to stay under the radar for as long as possible. What was the problem with lying if it was for a good cause?

So was born a very regrettable lifestyle habit: deception. My public practice of the faith did gradually fall off, so to what extent I actively mouthed things that I didn't believe, I can't say. The years all run together in my mind. But I certainly never spoke a word of what I truly believed during this time. My father's consternation steadily grew as he watched his son's slow-motion transformation from golden child to uninterested, angsty teen. Suddenly I had no appetite for going the extra mile in "Kingdom pursuits." The confessions dried up. I was reading on the family computer about why Noah's ark was bunk and glancing over my shoulder every now and then to make sure my parents couldn't tell what I was looking at.

The first shockwave this new outlook produced came at a district convention in Huntsville. I was able to room with one of our older friends, who gave me some alcohol. By some turn of events, this fact was leaked to a friend's girlfriend who would certainly report me to the elders (or so I was convinced). So I did the smart thing and beat her to it. I remember drawing a picture of a shot glass and passing the note to my mother during one of the sessions to explain what had happened. The fallout was immediate, and I was hauled before the elders when we all got back from the convention. My punishment was the stripping of my privileges (the microphone-handling duties that a male teenage Witness would be allowed to do in preparation for being appointed a ministerial servant). It would be the last time I would hold any formal position within the congregation.

Did I tell on myself because I still had lingering pangs of conscience, well-trained Witness that I was? I can pretty confidently say no. I had every reason to believe I would be snitched on, and that's because of the real informant culture that operates in the Witness organization. It's tell or be told on. Much of the material used by elders in their judicial hearings is extracted via confession-inducing questions like, "Are you sure there's nothing else you need to tell us?" These can pry open an anxious Witness and reveal a bevy of unexamined sins and accomplices that will require careful consideration by the elders. This secret police-type atmosphere spills over into all Witness relations. You don't hesitate to inform on somebody the moment you become aware of wrongdoing, or else you could in some way be held accountable for it.

A recent example will provide a case in point. My cousin Grayson who grew up a Witness was approached by his parents and told that they were leaving the religion quietly. He had given up much of his life to be a Witness and determined that he would stay a Witness whether they did or not. He called up a childhood friend in another state and confided in her about the whole thing. By the next morning this friend had already alerted her congregation elders, and news of the scandal spread like wildfire. I ask you, what would make a person turn traitor to someone's confidence like that except for either fear of punishment for not doing so, or a deep-seated and internalized police state mentality? Many such stories could be produced, I'm sure. When Witnesses see or discover someone else's sins, there's a feeling of guilt by association until the taint is purged by alerting the local elders. They are the only ones who can cleanse the community of sin, but to do so they must first know about it. The average Witness, then, is their eyes and ears. If you don't go unload your association with the sin before the elders, it could spread and grow and would certainly consume you as well, since you did nothing to stop it (you even hid it!). A well-functioning police state mentality diffused throughout a population can render the more intrusive techniques of surveillance superfluous.

So you can see, then, why I didn't give any would-be informants the pleasure of throwing me under the bus first. I proceeded to take my licks with a smile—this was, after all, the public demolition of the golden child persona, though many probably believed I'd just hit a snag and would return to form as I matured. Though I was demoted, I wasn't "out" as a nonbeliever.

I will admit that keeping secrets does have its own perverse pleasure, even though it undoubtedly corrodes the soul slowly. What was my endgame? What did I think was going to happen as I continued down this road? That the big reveal at the end of the show would bring everyone around? Or that the unbridled self-assertion of that final moment would be worth all the hiding, or, what's more, worth the almost sure suffering that would follow? Yet it was mostly teenage malevolence, I fear, that gave the whole thing a savor of adventure or even righteousness. It was probably for my own good that it seemed that way.

Friends, peers—like most teenagers, these were everything to me. I've often wondered if it's possible for a teen to be so quietly self-composed and confident that he is immune to this suffocating conformism. I certainly wasn't. Every element of my past (and present) was holding me back from what I considered normalcy, so I was bound and determined to assert my new identity, by any means necessary. I have to wonder, at this juncture, what my father could've even done. In all honesty, he probably acted in the best way he could. He maintained his rules and expectations, but he also didn't waste himself trying to enforce them at all costs. If I were to have asked if I could go to some worldly person's house for the night (likely to attend a party), he would've said, "Hell no"; but knowing that, I'd instead ask to go to my cousin's house. I had him there: how could he deny me the right to associate with my own cousin when my aunt and uncle were such good friends with him and mom? Once safely at my cousin's, we'd ask his mom if we could go over to a school friend's house. She was more lenient than my parents and would put up no resistance to our plans. We'd go to our friend's house alright, but that would be the staging point for attending a party (after securing some alcohol by hook or by crook).

Daddy could've said, "You're not seeing your cousin or any other of your lousy friends. You're sleeping each night in this house." But he didn't. I seem to remember curfew being a sticking point—on those nights when I didn't have authorization to stay somewhere else, did I usually make the curfew? I can't recall, honestly. Perhaps I didn't but just became an expert at sneaking in late. You know: turn the headlights off the truck and slowly creep down the gravel drive, parking as far away from the house as possible. Did he usually hear me, and just pretend not to? "I've got ears like a deer," he'd say. I'll probably never know. When my own son reaches this age, what will I do? Is it better to be permissive, so as to prevent him from thinking

DEDICATION, REBELLION, AND NEW GODS

you're hiding something good from him? Or could you actually prevent a boy from going down these paths if he otherwise would have? I'm sure it probably depends on the boy's personality and his level of stubbornness, and that a different touch is needed with each type. The mind of a teenager is a fickle, frustrating thing.

My mind was bent on what you might call the thrill of the night. Running with the pack, howling at the moon, that sort of thing. Of the core four, Jeremy was the oldest and the first of us to get a car. He had him a ninety-something Nissan Sentra. With the learner's permit you could get at age fifteen you could only have one passenger, and I remember, when the caravan was in transit, taking my turn as the passenger and thrilling to blaring noughties goth rock or alternative metal as we sped far too quickly around the curves of some back road. I think everyone needs a friend like Jeremy. That Sentra would be subjected to neon underglow lights, amateur two-tone paint jobs, and spray-painted rims before it was all over. Jeremy always had something new going: some new hobby, some new band, or some new scheme, and he'd sell you on it. You might sometimes roll your eyes, but it wouldn't be long before you'd want airbag suspension on your car too. (His second car, a '95 Mitsubishi Eclipse, could lift up and down, and had shaved door handles—inside and out. The remote control was absolutely necessary to get inside the car.)

We all got learner's permits and then licenses as soon as we came of age, and I remember it being a milestone when Levi, the youngest, got his license. His dad had restored and saved for him a 1966 Mustang, and so any errand that required the maximum amount of style was taken in that thing. My first vehicle was my uncle's old '94 Isuzu pickup, a stick-shift. Having a truck gives you some street cred out in the sticks (a manual transmission doubly so), so I was proud to drive it. It also meant, though, that junk hauling jobs became a frequent occurrence for me.

Our adventures mostly came into their own when Mike, who as I said was several years older than us, got married and bought a house. Marrying young is definitely something Witnesses do pretty often, and I think it's a good idea in general. This extended adolescence of frittering away your twenties on traveling and finding yourself is not societally sustainable. It seems to have led to more deeply ingrained patterns of selfishness in me now that marriage and family have finally come. But there's also an issue with people feeling pressure to marry when they're not equipped spiritually or culturally to actually sustain a marriage. When people hastily contract marriage nowadays, it usually ends in divorce (heck, when people date for ten years before getting married, it usually ends in divorce). That's because the self-sacrificial art of safeguarding a marriage has been lost. We're all affected by this in some way, but I think young Witnesses are especially blindsided by it. I of course attribute this to the aforementioned weaknesses in Witness spirituality. If there's not a mystical sense of being conformed to Christ through suffering, divorce can only be staved off by strong cultural taboos. That's certainly not to say marriage is some type of grueling trial to be endured, but just to say that any worthwhile, constructive endeavor is not going to totally tickle one's fancy 24/7. Yet it can be that momentary lapse in pleasure for many people that convinces them they've "made a terrible mistake" and need to get out. Marriage is one of those overarching societal goods that is bigger than all of us and our subjective satisfactions. If it falls, we all fall, though it may be unclear from each person's limited standpoint how "my marriage failing" is going to bring down the country.

But it does, because your life doesn't occur in a vacuum. The events of your life reverberate throughout your extended family, your workplace, your community, and ultimately to the nation and world. Even the things you don't do affect all the rest of us. Say you don't get married, and don't have kids (whether by choice or through force of circumstances). The kids down the street now are a bit lonelier. Fewer roots are put down, and the community loses stability. Of course, you personally may be unmarried and childless yet completely immersed in your community, and for that I would commend you. But the sad fact is that for many people it takes having a family for them to get involved.

You're not going to be able to see all these knock-on effects. Who am I hurting if I just sit and play Xbox all day? But this is why the Catholic tradition conceives of sin as a type of myopia or nearsightedness. You ignore the faith's prescriptions because they don't make sense to you or maybe even seem constricting. But then you wake up one day, and the Social Security system is collapsing and Medicare is bankrupt because *other people* didn't have enough kids that could've grown up and become contributors to the system. A system that is supporting healthier and longer living elderly people than it was ever designed to serve.

Anybody can recognize on a micro level that many times, we are our own worst enemies, individually. The Church offers an antidote to the micro level dysfunction that clears up a lot of macro dysfunction as well. We've completely rejected that medicine as a society, however, and so marriage has become a hollow shell of what it once was. There is no longer any cultural infrastructure that supports marriage, and so young Witnesses with high ideals (or maybe just burning loins) are left high and dry. My anecdotal experience was that many of the Witness marriages of the nineties and later were experiencing a similar divorce rate to those of the surrounding culture.

But boy were we glad when Mike got married and bought a house. It became the new base of our operations, the late-night hang-out, the site of pranks and jokes. Jeremy had another circle of friends from his high school who made home movies, edited them on a computer, and entered them in film festivals. He prevailed upon us to do the same, and "Geehoes" was born (the name, apparently, derives from *Jee-hoe*-vah's Witnesses, but it's hard to pin anyone down on that connection because of the irreverence implicit in such a name). Moviemaking became a much-loved pastime for us, and rewatching our work became a great way to reminisce in later years.

Our creed was barely Christian by this point. I of course was still doing the whole song and dance—three meetings a week, field service on Saturday, family study mid-week. But enforcement of these norms among the other boys was incredibly lax, even though they were all slower to shed their religious shackles. Javin came not far behind me, having somewhat absorbed atheism from my uncle, whose beliefs by that time weren't a secret. I remember when Javin and I cornered Levi one night at his house and gave him the book on Darwinian evolution we had read that we believed dismantled creationism. He was apprehensive at first—although he had been living, for all intents and purposes, like a nonbeliever, the prospect of facing down the logical implications of all that was none too appealing to him. But face them down and more he did, and increasingly so, as the years progressed.

Jeremy, though perhaps leading the most "normal" life of any of us, was the most resistant to any kind of formalized rebellion. I can't remember if we ever approached him explicitly about it. All I remember are some offhand remarks about how we "knew deep down it was the truth" and that our path betokened nothing good. To my knowledge he still identifies as a Witness.

With Mike and the older ones, this type of reckoning was totally out of the question, despite their somewhat rebellious or edgy posture within the congregation. They acted as paths to greater mischief for me regardless, so I didn't push it. This mischief chiefly began to crystallize around alcohol.

I'll never forget the first buzz I caught, from a beer we stole from Mike's stash: I felt the tingle spread throughout my body and a peaceful calm dawn in my mind. "This is what I've been looking for my whole life," I thought. "This will allow me to achieve my dreams."

I've explained some of the neurotic tendencies that cropped up in my tween years. Some of these tendencies also contributed to an awkward and anxious disposition. I describe it as an "awkwardness of the heart." It's not that I seemed strange in social situations (although I'm sure that occurred at times). It's more that I felt, at a deep level, uncomfortable in my own skin. Ill at ease. Never restful, never peaceful. Did religious fanaticism cause this? Not necessarily. My great-grandfather was a chronic alcoholic, and everything I've read admits that there's a genetic component to it. But it may be that the predisposition has to be activated by life experiences. As with most things, it's more complicated than just nature *or* nurture. It's definitely both.

And for me the nurturing of outsider status contributed mightily to my dis-ease with myself. As newly "liberated" in my mind, I was basically making up for lost time. I couldn't demonstrate my masculinity through public, open channels like sports or having a girlfriend (I wasn't allowed to date, since dating was only to be preparatory to marriage, and I wasn't old enough for that). So what was left were the secret, illicit channels that parents don't have to know about: drinking and partying. That first pulsating, floating high from that can of Miller or Bud or whatever it was (funny that I don't remember) proved to me in that moment that this was not just the only path open to me, but the very path *made* for me.

We gradually swore more and spoke more blasphemously, we sought alcohol however we could get it, and we pined away for the loss of our virginity like some pearl of great price. Once again, I was on the forefront of the rationalization matrix. If there was no God, and we could live as we pleased, then what should society look like? It sounds strange in this day and age, but the rural South in the early to mid-noughties still sort of felt like a conservative, evangelical place. I knew a couple of mixed denominational backgrounds—Baptist with Church of Christ—and this was something of a scandal in their families. Certainly to a fiery young atheist, small town Tennessee looked like a Christofascist state. Amazingly quickly, I radicalized into a liberalism of the most obnoxious type—that strain of elitist New Atheist snobbery that was in vogue back then. It asserted that science had disproved all these yokels' medieval beliefs, and so all their repressive and prejudiced customs needed to go by the wayside as well.

In fact, the problem seemed to me to be rooted in this whole "traditional culture" thing we had in the South and other "flyover" sections of the country. The accent, the cast of mind, the cultural associations—these were the fertile soil for beliefs still lingering in the South that needed erasure: a belief in different roles and affectations distinguishing men and women; a belief that gay marriage and abortion were wrong; and a belief in the supernatural, particularly Christianity. Traditional values grow best in a traditional, rooted culture. I sensed this and developed a hostility toward the South.

This is a great case study on the cultural genocide implicit in much of current-year liberalism. As far as roots, background, generational memory, etc., go, I am thoroughly Southern. I've got roots in the county I live in now that date to 1885 through my paternal line and other roots in the state of Tennessee going back to the 1780s. As an American I have veterans of all our wars in some corner or another of my family tree. I have every human and natural reason to feel thoroughly situated in a great historical chain with a definite and vibrant cultural heritage. Yet here I was as a sixteen-year-old in small-town Tennessee, cursing my own ancestors, trying to speak without an accent, and denigrating the ancient normalcy all around me.

I particularly took to the secularist version of the separation between church and state. I argued in our debate class on these grounds in favor of evolution, gay marriage, and abortion. Today it barely seems possible that these were edgy, minority positions at any high school. But the cultural force of evangelical Protestantism was still there in those days, though rapidly declining. Liberals in Bush's America could still cast themselves as beleaguered free thinkers surrounded by religious rubes.

Imagine the farce of me, the young man untutored in masculinity, viewing with contempt every religious person around him, spitting on his ancestors and heritage, and cloyingly seeking his fame in drunken spectacles at high school parties. That was the pathetic reality of it. To be fair to that wayward boy, some of the motives behind these actions yet held a germ of promise and came from a good place. My secular liberalism was, in the last analysis, an impulse toward truth no matter the consequences. I *did* wholeheartedly believe in it, and even though I wanted it to be true, it carried a lot of negative consequences that I was ready to endure. My independence of mind represented an openness to the radical honesty that would be necessary to save my life in later years.

High school, in short, was sneaking, always sneaking, to badness. There were great house and field parties I snuck to by way of my cousin, books about atheism and liberalism I snuck around reading at night, and a few girlfriends I snuck around to halfway date. At these parties and increasingly in more ordinary settings, if I could get ahold of enough alcohol, I would transform into my true self and wow the crowd. I was outgoing, confident, hilarious, and an insane dancer. One of my girlfriends was secured after an especially on-point performance at a field party one night. People talk about how it's a shame that young people feel pressure to drink and smoke to fit in. For me, it went deeper. I wasn't doing something I felt apprehensive about just to "fit in." I was using a magic elixir to become the person I'd always wanted to be: "the best version of myself," as the phrase goes.

This version did at times include things like embarrassing blackouts and crushing hangovers, it's true. But at this early stage, these things seemed a small price to pay, even somewhat amusing. The main problem was covering up the hangover symptoms from my parents. One time, I had a jug of Everclear in my trunk and had managed to drive myself from some remote outpost to Sunday morning worship at the Kingdom Hall. Bleary-eyed and exhausted, I must've looked like the walking dead. On this occasion, I correctly intuited during the closing song that I wouldn't be able to hold this one down. I fled to the bathroom and deposited the contents of last night's party into the first stall. Upon exiting I was confronted by my father, who obviously knew something was up. To my terror he needed to use my car, with the bottle of Everclear to be sliding around blissfully in the trunk all the while. He didn't happen to find it, miraculously, but the impression my bloodshot eyes left on him probably added to his growing impatience with my antics.

I needed my new best friend, and I wouldn't give him up for anything, no matter how risky things were getting. To illustrate: I was working on impressing a girl of high status at some party out in the country one night. I caved to pressure and smoked a Marlboro Light, the first cigarette I ever smoked, because she was smoking one. She asked if she could take me home. Everything was going great, but I realized midway through that I didn't have enough alcohol in my blood system or reserves on hand to last the night! My ease and confidence slowly started to evaporate.

After that, I decided to take my indispensable companion everywhere with me. Levi and I developed a system that included hiding a bottle of Wild Turkey 101 in a tennis bag in the woods at the end of his driveway. Then, on the way to school (we carpooled), the one not driving would dash into the woods, imbibe furiously, and then jump back in the truck for a super chill morning ride. We had a few close calls with that: office ladies catching whiffs of one hundred proof breath and reporting it to the principal, for instance. But in each case we somehow narrowly escaped.

Except for Jeremy, all of us liked to drink. But it started to become clear at this point that Levi and I were pulling away from the rest of the pack. This was especially true as I transitioned into college and Levi finished out high school. We operated on the "gloosh" system: how many "glooshes" (or large gulps of high-proof liquor) did you need before an event to get to that good-feeling place? It was our version of pre-gaming. And it was important to get the science down because both too few and too many glooshes could be disastrous. Too few and you just acquired incriminating booze breath with no real benefit; too many and you could become a blundering idiot and give away the whole game.

Meanwhile, high school was coming to a close. I came into my own senior year—the whole class did, really. We formed a cohesive body united by partying and our motto of "Oh-seven!" I got a date for prom and then stood her up because I got too drunk. I was living more "out loud" in many ways, mostly for the better. I found out my mom and her friends weren't planning on throwing us a graduation party, and when I confronted her she said she thought I didn't like stuff like that. Of course I liked stuff like that! I had fully evolved by this point from the straight-laced, baptized-at-age-eleven JW boy to a secular social striver. That reticence was a relic of the old me. We had the party for the 2007 JW graduates at the electric utility hall: Javin, me, my first girlfriend, and another girl we grew up with.

Big changes were happening, and I was excited about all of them. We had a pipe dream of establishing a "joint" house—joint being a double entendre for a house jointly occupied by all of us, and for the more delinquent meaning of the word. It is amazing to me how many hopes of a young man can be bound up in the prospect of unrestricted and uninhibited partying. Don't get me wrong—I still understand the appeal of a late night of spirits, spirited banter, and smoke, but back then it was so much more. I lived for it, probably more than most people. Most people, after all, don't feel like they were created with a bottle-shaped hole in their side. Intoxicated revelry made me happier than anything else in the world.

The revelry of those days seemed more wholesome (though that may be an abuse of the word) than the prescription drug-fests that kids indulge in nowadays. Being out in the sticks helped too, I think. There were fights occasionally, but nothing serious that I ever saw. The "oh-seven" cohort really came together senior year, and I finally felt like I had been a part of a large, public community. Like I had participated in society finally, after years of watching from the JW sidelines.

Chapter 4

Rebel Without a Prayer

Before we leave the country, I want to give a few impressions of that time and place. The memories are cemented in my mind against various backdrops, such as a late night at Jeremy's, laced with werewolf and ghost stories, tabletop games, and gas station pizza, set amid the night's enveloping darkness on the edge of town. Another one is a tree-canopied gravel road, the setting for a mad dash from a patio and a thunderous crash into a dry creek bed to wait out a police round up of underage drinkers, the cops having been called by one of them because someone "stole his stereo." Next is a wraparound porch illuminated by orange light encircled by branches and blackness. Beer cans line the handrail, smoke fills the air, and the only end to the night in sight is your own oblivion because the parents are away. I couldn't have conceived of a fresher heaven than that.

Many of my memories feature the inside of our Wal-Mart. So many late nights were spent roaming those twenty-four-hour brightly fluorescent aisles. Scenes from backroads and lightning bug-lit grassy fields, with the deafening roar of a chorus of croaks rising up from the earth. A McDonald's drive-through window at 10:30 p.m.; the gritty alleys behind the buildings on Main Street where we filmed that killer montage; breaks in field service at a rural gas station where I bought a bag of Skittles and the latest flavor of Mountain Dew.

Our congregation built a new Kingdom Hall during our high school years up on a large hill overlooking the lake. It was like something out of an old-time American barn-raising. We all came together for an intense two-week stretch to erect and finish the structure. The most vivid memory was the truss raising: men, women, and children pushed and pulled, standing the mighty pre-fabricated triangular arches into place. We cheered because it looked like a real building when we were done. I was on that hill more than the others (you can bet my dad was going to bust his tail for a project like that—and they needed him to, with his knowledge and experience), but everyone helped out. It was a great collective endeavor, one that changes you for the better in the process.

But that's how Witnesses used to build their Kingdom Halls (and maybe it still is). The main source of labor was the congregation itself, but it was partially under the direction of a more professional mobile building team. As with most things, it seems they do it this way for cost-cutting reasons, but the bonding experience through shared hardship is really the greatest benefit. That's something that I do miss—Witness congregations are run with such low overhead because you're expected to volunteer for everything. This could be seen as cynical and exploitative, but it also gives Witnesses a deep sense of ownership and accomplishment. Might you not look differently at the landscaping around your church if you were the one trimming it?

Moving along, college was on my horizon now. Despite the Witnesses' opposition to higher education, I was determined to go, and I heard in later years that my father secretly wanted me to so that I wouldn't have to work as hard as him to earn my living. But in the moment it seemed more a confluence of other factors. One of the older associates we had in the congregation had by that time successfully attended and graduated from college without losing his faith. He was quite liberal and quite loud on this point of college not being harmful, and I think he had an influence. The second is that I think Dad was picking his battles at this point. He knew he'd lost my mind and heart already, and I think he calculated that throwing down on this issue would probably only make things worse. Besides, what could I be exposed to academically or socially at this point that I hadn't already given myself over to? Lastly, I didn't ask for any help beyond a place to stay. I resolved to attend school in Middle Tennessee, which meant no room and board costs. At the right school I would be able to go with little personal expense. They never would've helped pay for it, but they weren't going to put me out on the street for it either.

My options were pretty limited, then, but at least I had a few. The private schools probably wouldn't have given me a free ride, but the reason I ultimately decided on Tennessee State University was because it was the only nearby school offering a city planning major. Technically it was urban studies, and it didn't actually exist yet, but I was assured that it would by the time I was ready to graduate. I had been interested in cities and buildings from a young age. I had most of the skyscrapers and their heights in Downtown Nashville memorized. One particularly exciting father-son outing I remember was getting to go to the observation deck of the L&C Tower (Nashville's first skyscraper) and then crashing a ritzy gala for the soaring Signature Tower, a proposal on Church Street by Tony Giarratana that ultimately got built but in scaled-back form. I'm still an urban planner today, and the reason why is that I believe the type of built environments we live and move in profoundly affect our quality of life. McMansions and Wal-Mart parking lots, while "functional," ultimately degrade us.

I did well in school and on standardized tests, so applying at a public college got me a full ride and then some. We made arrangements for me to stay during the week with my dad's parents who lived in West Nashville. I had been about as close as possible to my grandparents as a kid could be, and they had always spoiled me growing up. I foresaw an easy and convenient platform from which to launch big city partying antics. My cousin Javin, who also attended classes in Nashville, would be my running buddy.

Surprisingly, my grandparents didn't take too kindly to my all-night absences. My grandfather gave me an extremely stern talking to one morning after being out all night; he told me my grandmother had been so worried that she'd been unable to sleep while I'd been gone and that such behavior on my part was not to be repeated. That was the end of that, because I sure wasn't going to voluntarily live somewhere stricter than home. I moved back in full-time with my parents.

My parents, on the other hand, were moving in the opposite direction. Since some college classes are in the evenings, I was not terribly grieved, to say the least, when I was forced to schedule them during congregation meetings. And after this, if I remember correctly, even Sunday meetings became optional for me—I'm not sure how that happened. But I do remember Dad saying at one point, "I don't know why you don't jump at the opportunity to come to these meetings, if you're really looking for truth." I was, but he didn't know just how far afield I'd wandered looking for it.

I had gone much further than most people I knew. From a liberal Democrat I had slowly morphed into a revolutionary Marxist. But really, what else was there to be? I'd started out with the snobbish issues—issues that made me feel smarter and more cultured than all these backward, bigoted

Christians. You know—abortion, gay marriage, creationism, racism, separation of church and state, immigration/multiculturalism—culture war stuff. It's possible, if these are your chief concerns, to believe a better world is just a few Democratic Party victories away. However, there are certain tertiary economic issues that hang around the fringes of a mainstream liberal's consciousness. He certainly doesn't oppose or downplay them; he just doesn't think about them as much. These are things like the tanking middle class, stratospheric income inequality, the decline of unions, the lack of a living wage, the hollowing out of the industrial economy, etc. What might be called more "Old Left" priorities.

These economic issues were brought to the fore of my mind by the band Rage Against the Machine. I think it was my cousin who introduced me to them. They captured perfectly the youthful male rage one might feel toward an unjust world. And they talked about these *real* issues. Sure, they probably believed in all the culture war stuff the same as any leftist, but they sang about the workers and the oppressed of the world rising up and throwing off their shackles. They channeled the tradition of Marxism-Leninism and distilled it into a fine punk-rap-rock rage targeted directly at the powers that be. They introduced me to the dramatic, adventurous "arc of history" conception of the leftist revolution. It had all the power of a fairy tale struggle between good and evil and the added benefit of being real: I could become part of a great righteous struggle, and there was scientific reason to believe that it was all inevitably leading to a worker's world.

I maintain that if you're a liberal with one masculine bone in your body, you will eventually end up some type of socialist-communist-revolutionary. That impulse to *fight* for something (and I mean literally fight, not just fight in terms of marching and lobbying and begging) will push such a one to this conclusion. Mainstream liberalism is an incurably weak thing otherwise. The entire "civil rights" narrative and conception of America's history is one of throwing temper tantrums and crying for the capitalist state to throw you a social band-aid to make your miserable situation more tolerable. My youthful vigor could not long abide this neutered approach to political conflict. Those in power needed to be violently overthrown, or nothing would really change. Capitalism itself, not any of its excesses, was the problem. And if history taught us anything, it's that it wouldn't go quietly.

But on a more intellectual level, it was an actual reading of Marx that set the light bulbs off again in my head. It was this simple: labor creates surplus value, and owners (capital) steal that from labor because of an unjust legal system that allows capital to own the means of production. I of course didn't consider at all the risk-taking aspect of being an investor, or the surplus value that depends upon the oversight and control that management exercises. In any case, I could acknowledge these things while still arguing that a system where risk and decision-making are collectivized among the workers would be more just. In that sense I moved more in the direction of anarcho-syndicalism (through reading books like *Sin Patrón*),[1] but I never disavowed Marx, socialism, or communism. Judging by the number of Marxist and formerly Marxist countries, there was obviously something in that formula that appealed to people, and I didn't want to miss out on that.

Becoming a socialist also allowed me to re-evaluate a bit of my personal and familial identity and take some ownership and pride in it again. For several generations at this point my family had been pretty blue-collar. My dad's father being a salesman had been the most upper-middle class we'd gotten in recent history. The Marxist exaltation of the worker immediately awakened in me some dormant sense of family pride. Liberal Democrat Dustin was ashamed of his backward fundamentalist family. But Comrade Shane gloried in the true roughneck grit of his nobly oppressed proletarian parents.

One episode particularly captures this feeling and the growing rift between my cousin and me. Javin and I both loved Rage Against the Machine, we both loved to make edgy comments about the coming revolution, and we both loved to deconstruct religion. But my cousin tended much more toward nihilism than I did. In this he was simply more honest than me. Whereas I could plausibly swap out the eschatological hopes of my JW faith for the dialectical apocalypticism of Marxism and pursue both with childlike faith and optimism, Javin saw through it all to its bitter conclusions. No matter how cool or exciting or meaningful it might feel to discover the death of God and the coming battle for justice and utopia, ultimately, if God be truly dead, it's all for naught. Camus (who we dabbled in) was right then: the only question is why *not* commit suicide? At the time I took it as my cousin just being insufficiently radical: that maybe radical politics was just about the shock value for him, or that he was lazy and lacked the discipline to act on his convictions. We eventually had a disagreement, though, that hinted at the more Nietzschean direction he was heading.

1. Lavaca Collective. *Sin Patrón*.

Javin, Levi, and I were at Levi's house, and I started saying something about how under socialism or anarchism, blue-collar workers would be well off like white-collar professionals because all types of labor and the intelligence they require are equal. Javin cautiously took issue with this, and after an increasingly intense argument, he admitted that he thought maybe all our blue-collar dads didn't deserve to be rich because their skills just weren't that valuable to society. I couldn't believe what I was hearing. In my leftist worldview, the only reason factory workers didn't make as much as investment bankers was because the latter had rigged the system. When the owners and managers were done away with, most wage inequality would disappear, I believed. But what was more egregious about his comments was the insinuation that any type of human inequality could be based on something other than oppression. It smacked of Social Darwinism and the idea that some people were just stronger or smarter than others.

I've realized that I was ahead of my time with many of my sentiments. For example, I was always outraged that Confederate heroes still had statues up in the South. Heck, I correctly impugned the nation's founders as well: why were we celebrating these hypocritical slaveholders? Why was prayer allowed at football games, and why couldn't gay people marry each other if we really were this non-Christian, secular democracy? Why was whiteness the norm, standard, and default for discourse and perspective if "all men are created equal"? And how can women be equal if a Christian understanding of when life begins is being forced on them against their beliefs? Back in the late aughts, none of this was quite mainstream yet. However, I drew all these conclusions from Kerry-era liberalism, and the wider left (and society) would do so roughly a decade later. At the core of all this is a belief in absolute human equality: egalitarianism (not to be confused with the Christian belief in the equal worth of all humans before God; egalitarianism is more about function than nature). This is foundational to leftism, and the further left you go, the more pervasively it bleeds into every crevice of human existence.

Javin had threatened this core belief with his Nietzschean realism. Many liberals don't know how subversive Nietzsche is to the liberal worldview because they only know him as distilled through the postmodernists, or only as the "God is dead" evangelist. But he's very clear about his beliefs on fundamental human equality, and the implication of his thought is ultimately that the strong create the reality that the rest of us live with, and that this isn't good or evil—but since it *is*, we may just as well call it good. This has been the core conviction of the pagan right wing from the Nazis to the white nationalists of the Alt-Right.

But liberals don't really have a leg to stand on when arguing against that aspect of pagan thought. Despite their extreme moral convictions, most leftists would admit there's no ultimate grounding for their morals, either. "The Long Arc of the Universe" or "the Right Side of History" are more rhetoric and literary device than theological assertion. Even those who are "spiritual but not religious" in the end throw their hands up and admit there's no reason why "the greatest good for the greatest number" is some unchanging transcendental principle. If one act of unspeakable evil would save a thousand lives, would it be morally good to commit it? But then how would that be "fair," another leftist moral imperative?

Liberalism just replaces the *übermensch* with the *wille des Volkes* (otherwise known as 51% of the electorate). The proletariat will determine right from wrong because oppression will have become impossible without capitalism. As I write this I find it an almost comical belief today, and feel not a little embarrassment for having believed it. But it illustrates where I was coming from with Javin: people are naturally good when capitalism is not incentivizing them to be bad, and they're naturally equal when capitalism is not privileging some of them over others.

Javin stormed out that night, and I very nearly said good riddance to bad rubbish. I felt personally betrayed and offended on the part of our working-class family. After he left I reiterated to Levi the ideological rift we had just observed. We doubled down on our commitment to revolutionary ideals.

Levi and I had always been good friends, but as time went on this bond was cemented further. In addition to the above-mentioned beliefs, it increasingly seemed like he was the only one who loved strong drink as much as I did. As the fellowship splintered somewhat with the changes that came about in transitioning to college, Levi and I turned to less glamorous times with alcohol for our entertainment. We would just hang out, drink, and smoke. We'd travel backroads at night with a bottle of Wild Turkey 101, sometimes with Javin or someone else in tow; we'd "gloosh" Country Club one-hundred-proof vodka late into the night playing some meaningless PlayStation 2 game like *Tony Hawk* over and over; or we'd sit on the porch with a case of Natty Light and a couple packs of American Spirits if no parents were around. Drinking shifted from something I did to have a good time with people and more to something I did to have a good time, period. One time, after Levi had also gotten accepted to TSU (during my sophomore year), we drove all the way to Nashville for class, sat in the parking lot and said, "Do you really have to go to class today?"

"No. Do you?"

"No." And we turned around, drove back to his house, and started day drinking.

As a radicalized college student, I began to take steps to live in accord with my beliefs. I got on with the school newspaper and wrote a few articles. I covered one of the Nashville mayoral debates between Karl Dean (who would go on to win) and Bob Clement. Mr. Clement comes off like an idiot in my piece because he was the conservative. I got in contact with SDS (Students for a Democratic Society)—a leftist organization dating back to the sixties that involved itself in all kinds of revolutionary activities. I made a start at trying to get a living wage campaign going for the food and custodial workers on campus but didn't get very far with it.

I was increasingly impatient with how my parents were cramping my style at home. I tried to figure a way to make the "joint house" a reality, but without a sure commitment from one of the other interested parties, the idea remained a pipe dream. I attempted eventually to take things into my own hands. There was a Catholic Worker house in Nashville that was within walking distance of TSU. It was also a few blocks off a bus line that would drop me off at a Kroger grocery store. I had started working at the local Kroger probably a year before as a "courtesy clerk" (i.e., a bagger). I got a transfer approved to this inner-city Nashville store and announced to my parents that I was moving out. They tried to convince me that I wasn't ready; it didn't matter—I could taste freedom.

The guy that ran the Catholic Worker house had long ago abandoned the Catholic part, which of course didn't bother me in the slightest. Interestingly, he had actually known Dorothy Day, the famous foundress of the Catholic Worker movement who has a cause open for canonization, and he had converted to Catholicism under her influence. I didn't care for those religious associations but figured that as long as they were married to a sufficiently radical program that maybe they were tolerable. I moved in and he started demonstrating to me how the house ran. It was like an organic garden jungle, inside and out. The postage stamp-sized lot was planted over every inch with pesticide-free fruits and vegetables. I liked the idea of freedom from corporate agriculture, so this appealed to me. He further explained that I would be responsible for running the farm during the coming winter while he went back to Chicago to do plumbing or carpentry work (to earn the income that actually sustained the whole operation).

He bet on the wrong eighteen-year-old. After one grueling day at the new Kroger store and several nights of crushing homesickness, I broke down and moved back home. He admitted that this put him in a bind; he would have to scramble now to find another wintertime caretaker. But I was an impulse-driven boy, and my parents were still just willing to indulge me (but not for much longer). Luckily, my transfer hadn't even been processed yet, and so getting my old position back home was no trouble (I never got paid for that day of work in North Nashville, though).

The joint house was still a pipe dream, then, and we would have to make do with some level of parental oversight for now. Our latest home (since the beginning of high school) was in Levi's neighborhood, so I could walk to his house if necessary (and you can imagine it was very necessary many nights). I think it was around this time that I had another run-in with the elders that very nearly sealed my fate.

Our movie making capabilities had steadily increased over the years, and though we weren't as active as we once were, the projects we did do became more ambitious. Javin and I, along with two guys we went to high school with, decided to do a parody of MTV's *The Real World*, a reality show about strangers being forced to live together in a house. We called ours *Real World: East Hickman*, set in Eastern Hickman County, and populated by various redneck characters. (Hickman County is a poorer and more rural county than ours—Southerners love to trash other Southerners for being trashier than them.) In the show I played an abusive alcoholic father named Jonadab who smoked cigarettes, and the others had to live in my house. The one episode we filmed was predictably filled with drinking, smoking, cussing, and fighting.

We were proud of the final product, and so we uploaded it to MySpace. Of course it didn't take but a week or two for some scandalized JW to stumble upon it and report us to the elders (that whole informant culture I told you about). Soon my dad and the leading men had all seen the offending piece. "Yes, I've seen it," I remember my dad saying somberly when I asked him. It was something to be spoken of in hushed tones. Everyone was exasperated. I hadn't been in formal trouble with the congregation for several years, not since that drinking incident had occurred. People were starting to think I might just be getting back on track, or at least that I had halted my downward progress. Instead, video footage goes public of me screaming obscenities, drinking, and smoking the forbidden cigarettes.

I showed up at my judicial hearing at the local Kingdom Hall of Jehovah's Witnesses on something like a Tuesday or Wednesday night. The hearings were held in the back library room where a limited collection of Watchtower publications were kept (not too many—"old light," or doctrines that had been reversed or changed, were always needing to be weeded out, so the institutional memory represented in these libraries never dated back very far). I took my seat in front of the three elders, men I'd known almost my entire life, and after a few pleasantries and a prayer, the interrogation began. "You're not 21, yet it looked like you were consuming quite a bit of whiskey in that video."

"That was sweet tea," I explained. And that was true, though I believe we did have real celebratory drinks after we finished filming.

"You really looked like you knew what you were doing smoking that cigarette in the scene by the creek. That looks like something you've practiced quite a bit."

I had to tread lightly here. Being a smoker was surely a disfellowshipping (shunning) offense—but what about just smoking for a movie scene, or maybe just smoking a couple times out of curiosity? "I'm not a smoker," I said. And that was true, if you define smoker as someone who smokes daily or on a regular basis. I only smoked sometimes, when I drank in a safe environment. "It wasn't hard to make it look real. We wanted it to be more authentic," I explained further.

I'm not sure why I parsed my words so—I was ready and willing to unload my disbelief on them as a defense for my actions, fully expecting disfellowshipping as a result. I guess it's just that I didn't want to be canned for something as ignoble as smoking.

"Dustin, why would you think it wise to do something like this? You know Jehovah's laws against smoking."

I considered how to say the next part. "I guess I'm just not sure about this whole thing, and so making a movie with smoking in it just didn't seem like a big deal."

"You mean not sure about *the truth*?" They weren't ready for that one.

"Yeah." I swallowed. "I've been reading and studying about biology, and it appears to me that a lot of the arguments and statistics in the publications are mistaken and sort of misleading."

And so then came the proof texting. I'd show a bogus claim in the anti-evolution JW book, and then we'd argue about it, or they'd bring up some flaw in my logic or reading of the source, and I'd try to soft-pedal a defense without looking too committed. Once you get into a discussion like this with a judicial committee, there's a very small, always diminishing window through which to escape without being disfellowshipped. It can vary widely, but the elders view the committed questioner or doubter as a cancer to be removed from the body politic. But, technically, just experiencing doubts isn't enough to incur this judgment.

As the inquiry continued, I became steadily more obstinate. In my mind I had already missed the window: like I said, it's small, and I'd heard of being disfellowshipped for less.

Finally, the deliberation time came. "If you would, please wait outside. We'll call you back in after we've come to a decision." I stepped outside into the parking lot. It was dark and cool by now. I thought about everything in my life that was about to change. I still lived at home, so I'd be able to speak to my parents and sister, but being invited to larger family gatherings at my grandparents' would cease. And once I moved out, the break with even my parents would be total. In my youthful enthusiasm and self-righteousness, I'm sure I didn't appreciate the magnitude of what was about to happen. There's a romance about being a martyr for truth that bewitches all people, even atheists. My friends would stick by me, at least. None of them were baptized except the older two, and so they were immune from this whole circus. As I waited in the still evening air, I was nervous, but not frightened.

One of the elders opened the door and motioned me back in. I entered the chambers and took my seat once again. "Well," one of them said, "we're not going to disfellowship you."

Shock and relief spread over my face. I probably said something like, "Oh, thank you."

"But understand how dangerous of a position you put yourself and the congregation in. We think, however, that you are just sincerely confused and struggling, and we want your dad to study with you."

"Thanks; yes, I want to study. I just want to know the truth." My eager words seemed to confirm their judgment.

"If that's truly the case, then you'll find it, if you keep your heart honest."

I briefly took in the sight of these three older men, men of great power in this context. I'd known each of them for at least a decade; they'd watched me grow up; they'd likely cheered my accomplishments and mourned my falls. I looked for just a second into each of those men's eyes and saw a paternal mercy that I'd totally discounted in all my calculations about the rules and protocols concerning crime and punishment. These men knew me, and they wanted to hope for me. It was undeserved kindness shining through the cracks of this absurd power structure. I have those three men, three fathers, really, to thank for five more golden, irreplaceable years with my family. For the reckoning, forestalled by these merciful judges, was as inevitable as it was terrible.

Studying with my dad took the form of me trying to innocently bring up objections to his beliefs and letting him knock them down without too much pushback from me. That's the problem with forced re-education: you can never be sure if the person you're trying to brainwash is ever truly convinced. How could I really engage in debate on these topics when a too aggressive posture might land me back in a judicial committee hot seat, and this time with the consequences all but certain? So I was always stopping just short of what I wanted to say, or leaving things too devastating to his arguments unsaid (or things too revealing of my true disposition). I was trying to lead him to my views without owning my views.

The only truly frank conversation we had was *before* the judicial hearing, when I thought all was lost anyway. We were driving along past a Church of Christ, when he began to question me. "Why would you create a video like that? Don't Jehovah's laws mean anything to you?"

"If you doubt the entire thing," I said pensively, "then it really doesn't seem like a big deal."

"Doubt the whole thing? You mean like the truth, God's organization? What you did is wrong according to the Bible, not just the organization, if you're doubting that."

"I'm talking about the whole thing, not just the organization."

"You mean to tell me you're an atheist or something?" he asked, stunned.

Well, here it was. Might as well go all in. I anticipated it coming out at the trial anyway, and the course of conversation seemed to demand it at this point. "I've been studying Darwin and evolution, Dad," I said. "There's proven science behind all this, and all the publications that argue against it use misquotes and misrepresentations to make their case."

That last part didn't register with him. "So you really believe all life, the whole universe, is one big cosmic accident that runs on blind chance?" He had skipped the noise and cut straight to the heart of the matter.

Well, yeah, is what I was thinking. What else would it mean? But I didn't answer quite like that. I had to give it a little finesse. I was a thoroughgoing materialist at this time, meaning that I did believe everything was just atoms bouncing around and reforming. Yes, one day we would all be dead meat, or dead dust, our lives and consciousness extinguished. I tried to blunt the force of this traumatic conclusion by watching nature documentaries, basically.

It's strange that learning about the intricacy and beauty of nature makes scientistic atheists feel better about their bleak worldview, but it does. I think it's a combination of two factors: one, appreciation of nature produces feelings of wonder, gratitude, and peace within nearly everyone, regardless of whether you think there's someone to be grateful to for it or not. Second, evolution seems true, or at least the people who produce these materials make it seem true, and so consuming them confirms the already held belief.

I tried to explain this to Dad, about how nature was so awe-inspiring, and yet how science had explained it all to us, and that even if it all was ultimately meaningless, one could derive subjective satisfaction from existence, and that we'd all be better off if we just accepted that. Of course he wasn't satisfied by any of that—who would be? It's why very few of these "New Atheist" types still exist. I didn't realize it at the time, but I was swept up in a larger current of thought (that has thankfully dwindled to irrelevance) that people like Richard Dawkins were spearheading.

Nothing but a science textbook could've been true to me back then, so the Bible didn't have a chance. Pick almost any part of the Old Testament, and a straightforward, literal reading of it will appear impossible in the light of modern science. But that's probably not how it was meant to be read, and that's certainly not its primary purpose. I have no clue how Jonah lived three days in a fish's belly. Maybe the whole thing was a big miracle, with God suspending several laws of physics at once. I don't know if Methuselah took 969 full trips around the sun, or if he just lived a really long time, or if he was just a really impressive man. It doesn't, in a sense, matter. One first needs to take off the reductionist, materialist lenses before even approaching the Bible.

But New Atheist teens can't be told that because very few of them have enough self-awareness to take a step back from their views and think in terms of paradigms. For me, it was enough to demonstrate that animals living prior to Adam and Eve had sharp canines (meaning they ate meat when meat was only supposed to have been eaten *after* Adam and Eve fell) to conclusively prove that the Bible was complete fantasy. Never once did I consider that such simplifications of the richness of reality were value judgments of the most arbitrary kind.

Dad wouldn't have phrased it that way, but his instincts told him as much. He was patently stunned that his son could've fallen for *atheism*. And valiantly did I try to persevere in that fall, despite the growing emotional toll. Have you ever tried to believe for a prolonged period of time that, one day, not only you and everyone you know, but the planet itself and the entire solar system would be consumed in a fiery conflagration, with all life and existence as we know it blotted out—not a trace, not even the possibility of a fragment of a memory, left behind to show for it? That literally, everyone and everything you know and that even can be known will one day be completely obliterated? That life is really just a cruel joke, a great illusion—sound and fury, signifying nothing? Can you believe that for very long if you really understand what you're believing? Many find it unbearable, and that number would soon include me.

It wasn't too long after the hearing—I don't remember exactly when, maybe a year?—that I began to soften my views on the supernatural, death, and the afterlife. Religion was still bunk, of course, but I started toying with the idea that perhaps there is something like "soul" in the universe, and that just maybe this substance leaves an "impression" that is enduring. Still thoroughly materialistic, you see, but reaching for some solution that would make the problem of death more tolerable. Interestingly, the main bit of evidence I marshalled in support of this point was the widespread anecdotal evidence of ghost sightings.

Maybe it seems strange for a hard-nosed materialist to become open to the reality of things that go bump in the night, but you have to admit: ghosts are a pretty universally attested phenomenon. As an evidence-based guy, I couldn't ignore this. Was it really like the atheists said it was, that all throughout history, everybody who ever saw a specter was hallucinating or just making it up? That seemed unlikely to me. My second cousin Devin, for instance, was an ex-Jehovah's Witness who was now officially uncommitted to any belief system. Maybe he believed in God still, but I doubt he'd fight you over it. He messed around with a Ouija board a few times at the behest of some friends, probably because he didn't believe in it, and experienced inexplicable phenomena: a flying object, berserk dogs, and impossible smells. This was someone I trusted deeply, someone with no agenda or axe to grind, simply recounting what he'd seen. Dogmatic atheists out there will have a battery of explanations, I'm sure, but I think they're kidding themselves. I know when I've actually seen something and when I only *think* I've seen something. You may be able to blame some ghost sightings on overactive imaginations, but to conclude that all of them are either lies or delusions beggars belief. I concluded that there must be *something* "super" natural in the universe. Maybe it was something we couldn't measure yet. Or, perhaps some type of "spiritual" realm did exist—I figured ghost sightings and Ouija boards were about as close as we could get to it, so why concern myself too much? The point was, now that I'd come down from the atheist ledge, I could still indulge whatever lifestyle I wanted but without all the crippling despair and hopelessness. That's what agnosticism is: a big, soupy, lukewarm bath of cheap comfort. Live as you will, there's still no capital-"g" God—just a vague netherworld that you can affix all your existential hopes and dreams to. Since no one knows or could know anything about it, you're free to build it into whatever you like. I couldn't accept the annihilation of my individuality and that of everyone I love, so my vision of the afterlife naturally contained the spiritual part of us that people see as ghosts, and that was all the spirituality I needed. Or was it?

Chapter 5

The Darkness Shattered

As my beliefs and I attempted to mature, I continued to work at Kroger, where I would work for four and a half years, all through college and a little after, and I thoroughly enjoyed my time there. Grocery stores are the crossroads of community and, if you think about it, the source of life.

Working at a grocery store (especially cashiering) is like working on an assembly line, but if you can motivate yourself to engage with and talk to your customers, you'll enjoy it more. The best way to view others while doing service sector work is to see them in the same type of detached yet interested way you would view characters in a novel. People in novels are just as flawed as people in real life, yet the former fascinate us and the latter annoy us. This is because we view people in real life through a self-interested lens. People in books and stories can't frustrate your plans or stymie your selfish will like flesh-and-blood people you meet in your daily life can. The mystical vision the saints have been given is to see objectively, or to see people as they are, not as they affect us. That requires the type of Christian detachment that, rather than leading to indifference, is actually the precondition for the purest type of love. It's empathy to the very last drop of the word. And it's the foundation for the kind of joyful, spontaneous, fearless lives that only saints can live.

I didn't have holy detachment, joy, or fearlessness in my life. I lived hedonistically, and not just with regard to fleshly pleasures. My life was a series of events with various threat levels attached: threats to my comfort, my ego, my fortunes. It was fundamentally reactive. I wasn't necessarily miserable because there were enough periodic dopamine hits to look forward to. I wasn't happy either, though: I was *after* things, things that would make me happy, I believed.

While at Kroger, I finally found a girl I really liked who also seemed to like me. Her family ran a shop across from my store. This poor woman probably didn't know what hit her. I say that, not because my dysfunction wasn't apparent, but because we were married something like a year after we met.

Your memories are calibrated to your level of maturity at the time, so I guess it shouldn't seem odd to me that I remember the situation as seeming normal, but it was anything but. How else to explain her agreeing to a third date after being subjected to the "drunken chauffeur" on the second? But how else was I to go a-courtin' with my best foot forward? If, when drinking before a date, I occasionally overshot the mark and showed up a little sloppy, that was just the cost of doing business. I liked me better buzzed, and I believed other people did too, though I couldn't always remember their reactions. It's amazing to me how few people called me out during these years for being publicly intoxicated. As a drunk, you start to think that means people don't know—but they do. I can detect alcohol on someone from a mile away. But then again, I rarely say anything either.

I think she did try to confront me a few times about me showing up to dates drunk. I don't remember how I responded, but I do know that stopping was not an option. I was doing it for *her*, so that I could be the carefree, outgoing guy everybody loved. But the farce was about to exceed everyone's expectations.

When not with her, I was at Levi's, blacking out after mindlessly playing *Tony Hawk's Underground* for PS2 late into the night. Some nights my parents demanded I not stay overnight, so I'd have to walk or drive the half-mile back home, drunk either way. Little can I convey the satisfying peace that these rituals produced in me: the fiery warmth of the hundred-proof vodka spreading across my chest, the familiar virtual landscape and repetitive soundtrack of *Tony Hawk*, and the conversation with a kindred spirit that helped me make sense of it all. The mental pathways being solidified could've kept me in thrall to liquor for years to come. These are commonly referred to as triggers by addicts, but they're more like well-worn neural road ruts radiating security and comfort. Their impressional force can overshadow any and all other considerations almost totally. They seem to have no connection to the negative consequences that result from them: they're too good, too pure, too exactly-what-I-need to be tarnished by such complications. Levi got it as well, and so our camaraderie was solidified.

Sometimes memory would fail me at the end of such a night, and I'd startle to find myself back at home the next morning. Was my car outside? I came into the kitchen one time and was presented with the sight of my father holding up a deformed wedding band. I had childishly bought a ring for a hundred bucks because me and the gal had talked about getting married. "What is this?" he asked me pointedly. "I found this in the gravel driveway outside."

I gasped. "That's mine! I didn't realize I'd dropped it!" I exclaimed as I grabbed it.

Mom and Dad looked at me with disgust. They knew exactly why I had lost it and exactly why I had no memory of losing it.

"I hope she knows what she's getting with you," my father said, grimacing.

I had no reply, but I didn't think I needed one. Just an honest mistake, really, that anyone could've made. People drop things all the time! The fact that a drunken blackout was involved just made it *seem* like it was some particularly egregious failing on my part. Anyway, I could buy another, and she'd never know. Problem solved.

There wasn't much time for that, though. To outsmart the ever-constricting parental anaconda, Levi agreed to come over to my house instead of me going over to his, which my parents were beyond suspicious of by this point. Sure, it would be harder to smoke cigarettes at my house (and the stakes for getting caught much higher), but we would be able to drink fairly safely in my room.

We successfully carried out this plan a few times and in the process built up a mighty stash of empty cans and bottles. I had these stored away in a trash bag under my bed. I didn't sweat too much about how I would get rid of them: I'd just wait until both parents were gone and then run them out of the house to some public trash can. My chance came one Sunday while they were off at the Witness meeting. I got distracted somehow, though, because I was also heading out on some other errand. Just before I was ready to head back home, a sickening realization hit me: I had left the two large trash bags loaded down with beer cans and vodka bottles just lying on the kitchen counter—I'd brought them that far but forgotten to bring them out the rest of the way!

I raced home in a panic. If it were a normal Sunday and my parents had come straight home from the Kingdom Hall, then all was lost—they'd surely be home by now. I hoped beyond hope that maybe they'd stopped somewhere on the way home, or gone to lunch first. The presence of the family car in the drive, however, soon filled my heart with despair.

I entered and gingerly greeted them. "Oh, you got that trash I was meaning to throw out," I said when I saw the bags missing.

"Yes, and for the last time," my dad said sternly. Momma looked glum. "You're out of this house, Son," he said. "Pack your stuff; I'm changing the locks."

I was dumbfounded. Was he really going to do it? But of course he would, and why shouldn't he? For years I had insisted on living the way I wanted, his rules or beliefs be damned. Sometimes secretly, sometimes openly, but it was an open secret at this point. I'm honestly surprised he let it go on as long as he did. But there was no other possible conclusion to this whole test. We both believed wholeheartedly in the truth of our respective paradigms. A showdown was assured, and of course he would win: he had the house, the money, and the authority. I had taken more of a bandit-type approach: I knew all this, but I figured I'd try to last as long as I could before the inevitable.

So ultimately I wasn't shocked, and I mounted very little resistance. In one sense there was relief. Finally, something would be forcing me to get out on my own. And this would also force the issue between my girlfriend and me: if we were going to move in together, we'd have to get married first. Shacking up was a disfellowshipping offense.

You may be asking why clear evidence of drunkenness wasn't. And to that I can only answer, once again, mercy. My parents could've turned me in for drinking underage and gotten me shunned instantly. But like those three elders from my last run-in with the law, they didn't. It surely wasn't because they weren't mad—they were livid. But no matter their regret over my crimes, at the end of the day they just didn't want to shun me. I think they hoped I would come to my senses before it came to that. They were prepared for it, for sure, but they weren't going to hasten it. But Dad needed to kick me out. He needed to be able to wash his hands of it and let fate take its course. My sins would catch up to me in God's time.

In the meantime, I needed a place to land. Levi's parents agreed to let me stay with them for a limited time. I only needed about two weeks, during which time I signed a lease on an apartment and got married at the county clerk's office. We called my mom that morning and told her our plans, causing her to collect two of my aunts and drive up to Nashville in a great huff to witness it while complaining about not being given enough notice. We had the reception at the White Castle on Charlotte Pike.

It may seem hard to believe that the marriage could've been even more pathetic than the courtship, but so it was. The first issue was that we moved into a low-rent ten-unit apartment building in a (then) seedy part of town. The building was inhabited mainly by other alcoholics, which didn't take long to figure out. There was a common courtyard that backed up to a roofing company's building on one side. Oh, how many nights did we all gather there, laughing, cussing, threatening one another, the alcohol flowing freely and the cigarette smoke choking the air! Everyone else was quite a bit older than me—from their late thirties up into their fifties. Everybody had a reason for being there: Mortimer had his license revoked, so he had to keep his factory job across the street or he'd be up a creek. Luke had played the Stage downtown before and had done some record work with someone from a major country act, but that guy wasn't returning his calls as of late, and so he was biding his time working at the car wash. Ellen did pretty well for herself but had a little coke habit that we weren't supposed to know about. And Bud was a songwriter from North Carolina who just didn't care about getting ahead.

It's amazing to me how strong the bonds between revelers can feel. There's such a kindred spirit and a refreshing transparency that taps something at your core. It can seem like such people are your closest friends in the world. But there's a very utilitarian underbelly to it. The other drinkers are to some extent props: incidentals to the scene, necessary but not sufficient. They form the backdrop to the true relationship that's taking place: the one between the addict and his drug. I didn't want to hang out with these people because I valued them as people; I wanted to hang out with them because they were involved in the same deadly dance that I was. Take away the booze, and the lazy hours spent together would've ceased.

I don't want to come across as a teetotaling puritan on this point. Very frequently, a ritual like lighting up or sharing a few drinks can be the perfect social lubricant to help people get outside themselves and bond over a shared experience. The "third party" of alcohol can take the pressure off the interaction and keep it from descending into mutual navel gazing. Addicts are different, though. It's more like we just need an audience for the unfolding of our relationship with alcohol. In some ways it doesn't matter who that audience is.

The friendships formed when people are using one another in this way can be real, though. I am still in touch somewhat with Mortimer and consider him a friend. But in the midst of addiction, the drink will always come first. Friendships can be built around strong drink, but their strength is only proved in sobriety. Until then they're just marriages of convenience.

And revelry was very convenient at that time in my life. I could finally do exactly what I wanted, when I wanted, as long as I respected three checks on my behavior: my work schedule, my school obligations, and my wife's level of fed-up. Bless her heart, I was given more grace than I ever deserved with that last one. Imagine trying to go to bed because you've got to get up and go work ten hours the next day, and at about one or two in the morning, a drunk man reeking of cigarette smoke loudly fumbles his way through your house and into your bed before vomiting all over the place where you sleep. You then have to get up, clean the mess, and explain to him after you get home from work the next day why there's a big stain on the mattress.

I would get blackout drunk at least once a week. And she cooked and brought in most of the money (she was full-time and I was only part-time because of school). Unequally yoked is an understatement. Filled with remorse and a surge of gratitude, I would beg for forgiveness when the bleakness of midmorning finally found me conscious. It was the least I could do.

An alcoholic has two minds: one is present at these comparatively rare moments of lucidity, when he sees clearly and will repent in sackcloth and ashes. He will pledge, swear, declare blood oaths that he is done, and that he will never hurt those he loves ever again. He at least will try to put in place some type of safeguard: I'll only drink on weekends; or, I'll only buy a six-pack; or, no more hard liquor, just beer from now on. He means these promises sincerely.

But there's another consciousness lurking inside him. This other man can awaken at the slightest provocation. A man not a day into a solemn oath can catch a glimpse of a friend or even a stranger enjoying a drink and instantly transform, the seed having been irrevocably sown. This is good-time Charlie, bane of wives, children, and loved ones everywhere. The madness will not abate until another catastrophe has left him broken and ashamed.

It's really the case that alcoholism is just a very stark and poignant picture of sin generally. Sin is a form of madness, a tragic lack of perspective, as St. Augustine says. We overemphasize minor goods and underemphasize major ones. The minor good of efficiency causes me to get short or angry with a loved one, jeopardizing the major good of our relationship or the person's feelings. The minor good of a novel sexual experience causes a husband to trample the major goods of marital fidelity, honesty, loyal love, and his children's well-being, since children suffer the most from divorce. The common theme is misplaced priorities. That's where an alcoholic's benders come from: he feels the *joie de vivre*, he worships the ease and comfort that flood his soul when once the demon liquor takes hold of him. In that moment of temptation, it is all he can see. Then, with each subsequent drink, his faculties of judgment break down further and resistance becomes literally impossible. What couldn't be resisted in sobriety has no chance of being withstood under the influence.

I never drank alone. But I also never had to. With my neighbors, the bacchanalia could be enjoined several times a week, and all weekend. Things occasionally got out of hand: someone had to be put in his place, or someone would call the cops. Sometimes the few neighbors that didn't participate would complain about our noise or mess. After one night with the boys from back home, a particularly clueless bumpkin I had invited decided to unleash a golden shower over top of the balcony railing, apparently forgetting that he wasn't on his grandparents' farm anymore. The downstairs neighbor was enjoying the day's first cigarette when a yellow mist descended down before his face, like Jove upon Danaë. "What the #@*%?!" ricocheted across the concrete block walls, causing the urine stream to abruptly stop. The boy ran inside and put his head down in shame as my outraged neighbor tried to break my door down. We had to wash the sidewalk with soap to keep the man from lodging a formal complaint with the landlord.

Another time a second-floor neighbor pushed an old couch off his balcony into the dumpster below. The couch was too big for the container, so the garbage truck would pass up our dumpster when it came by. After a couple weeks, the household garbage had so piled up in and around the receptacle that people were starting to complain of the smell and saying that it was attracting rats. The instigator of all this then decided to clandestinely take matters into his own hands. When no one was looking one Saturday morning, he lit the sofa on fire. It burned, all right—and too well. The flames jumped up higher than he had anticipated and began to lick the apartment building. Sheer pandemonium broke out as the blaze grew. It was slightly intoxicated me who finally called 911. That day Levi had planned to come hang out and was bringing his girlfriend up to see our place for the first time. "It's in a rough part of town, but nothing too crazy," he had reassured her. They pulled up to the sight of police and fire fighters surrounding the dingy two-story apartment building as a dumpster fire raged and terrified residents spilled into the streets.

Surprisingly, it was during this time of increasing debauchery and irresponsibility that I began to warm up to the idea of organized religion. Previously I had abandoned straightforward atheism in favor of an indeterminate but more comforting agnosticism. I took the next step toward religion, but for political rather than spiritual motives. My Marxism and anarcho-syndicalism had taken a more populist flavor lately. How could we accomplish the real goals of the revolution, like abolishing hierarchy and capitalism, if we were constantly alienating the bulk of the proletariat (which in Tennessee consists heavily of socially conservative "rednecks") with our stances on ancillary cultural issues, like gay marriage and abortion? Of course *I* was in favor of both of those things, but having left the weak sauce reformist Democratic Party agenda for the true meat of revolutionary Marxist politics, I didn't see why these lesser, more symbolic issues should be kept around as stumbling blocks to our otherwise natural constituency. Now, I'm aware that, in the year of Our Lord 2023, such "cultural" issues have been unmasked as central to the progressive and left-wing political program. But back in 2009, many on the left still seemed to view culture war issues as a distraction from the class war. Winning that epochal struggle was supposed to eventually fix many of the retrograde tendencies of the workers, much the same way it would fix the problem of the heavy-handed state (both would "wither away"). Why then alienate so many potential allies with issues that scarcely affected the exploitative economic conditions they faced?

I attended the 2009 International Socialist Organization's conference in Chicago that year, hitching a ride up with some Wobblies (Industrial Workers of the World, or IWW, members) from points farther south. The ISO was a Trotskyist organization associated with the Fourth International and some guy named Tony Cliff in the UK. They were famous for their characterization of the Soviet Union as "state capitalist" after the death of Lenin and expulsion of Trotsky. This group was in contrast to outfits like *People's World*, which didn't entirely reject communism and continued to support "communist" governments like the People's Republic of China.

Marxists (and really revolutionaries of all sorts) are a lot like Evangelical Protestants. There's a central authoritative text, usually the writings of Marx or some downstream founder, that acts like the Bible does within Evangelicalism. Everyone accepts it as self-evident, but no one agrees on what it means or how it should be implemented. The tired trope of "real communism has never been tried" applies with varying degrees of accuracy to each group. As I said, the ISO accepted as canon Marx and all the writings and actions of Vladimir Lenin and Leon Trotsky and the general conduct of the Soviet Union until Stalin's takeover (meaning basically that the whole project went to hell in less than a decade). Other groups accept the subsequent Stalinist regime and similar governments as legitimately socialist/communist and work hard to spin the actions of those governments in a pro-democratic way. Yet others reject every actual victorious socialist revolution as having instantly spiraled into tyranny and therefore straightforwardly say, "True communism has never been tried." A group's position on these questions will determine what other materials they consider authoritative. Then of course there are anarchists, who reject the whole Marxist framework and believe Marxism is the reason every victorious socialist revolution led to a repressive state. They have their own canon, heroes, and foundational myths.

Surveying all this, I chose the ISO because I wanted to believe that the reason communism had turned sour so quickly was not because of any inherent problem in the theory itself but because Stalin was so evil. He evilly subverted the good and heroic movement of Lenin and Trotsky. Although this ignores the massacres and repressions of Lenin and Trotsky (the Kronstadt sailors, the establishment of the Cheka, etc.), the ISO had semi-satisfactory explanations for these things. But I wasn't super sectarian about most of it. I was drawn to the libertarian cooperative model of anarchism more than I was to the dictatorship of the proletariat idea, but at the end of the day, if Marxism represented a proven strategy for accomplishing the revolution, I'd grab a red flag and call myself a Marxist.

I put my ideas into practice when I got back from the convention. I learned that there had been a "Populist Party" in Tennessee in the 1890s that had briefly challenged entrenched wealth and power in the state. With those farmers of yesteryear as my inspiration, I wrote up a bunch of articles (Levi also contributed one) spelling out a type of modern-day populist manifesto with obvious anarcho-syndicalist undertones. I called it *The Midstate Populist* and got something like a thousand copies printed on newspaper by a printer in Lebanon. My plan was to go door-to-door handing them out, with the goal of building up a local revolutionary party in West Nashville.

The paper's content was strictly economic—no culture war distractions. In fact, I even referenced the Bible and Christ's words about the rich man and the eye of a needle (Luke 18:25). As a "populist" (and not in the right-wing sense in which that term is used today), I saw no issue with church-going, if that's what the people were about in my local area, and I actually saw many anti-wealth elements within Christianity that could be very helpful to me. I hadn't gotten much buy-in from my fellow socialists at the convention with my talk about dropping the push for gay marriage and abortion. They seemed to sense (correctly, as it turns out) that there was something reactionary about such a strategy. But this was 2009 rather than 2019, and so free speech and thought were not yet dead letters on the left.

I would drop off a few copies of my paper at grocery stores and laundromats, but when it came to house-to-house distribution, I found that a good buzz really made the whole process easier; otherwise, it was such a strange thing to do that the awkwardness could be overwhelming. However, it was hard to maintain my high in the blazing heat, traipsing about on foot as I was. I only went out twice knocking on doors. At this point in my life, I was no Lenin. (Did Lenin have to pre-game before his "all power to the Soviets" speech in 1917?)

Paradoxically, because of all this, I found myself exploring the idea of going to church. Church seemed to me part of the infrastructure of proletarian life, and so any revolutionary who wanted to reach the people needed to ingratiate himself within a church, I reasoned. There were also vague stirrings in my soul toward some sort of spirituality. One day, when my curiosity got the best of me, I picked up Thomas Merton's *The Monastic Journey* from a local used bookstore. Now remember, I in no way considered the Bible or the Catholic Church uniquely true or divine in their foundations. I had merely started to believe that maybe the great religions of the world were collectively on to something that a booze-soaked sot like me could benefit from. And I extrapolated that if I were going to pursue a religion to socially benefit from church membership, it would help if it were the popular kind, which meant Christianity.

But there was a little snag in my planned embrace of the people's religion: I was finding myself, mostly unintentionally, drawn toward Roman Catholicism. If you're in the North or West this may sound strange, but in the South (particularly the more upland or Appalachian parts of it like Tennessee), Catholicism still has something of the savor of a foreign object. It's nowhere near like it used to be, like when the second Klan was big in the early twentieth century, but it's still rare enough that if your main concern is social acceptance, you may just want to settle for High Church Episcopalianism.

My wife and I tried to attend Park Avenue Baptist Church a few blocks away at first. We met several wonderfully kind people. The church seemed to have an issue with attracting younger people, though. I think someone even asked us why we didn't try out their sister church, which was one of those rock band megachurches that met in a "worship auditorium."

I was conflicted for a few reasons: one was that I had this image in my head of the traditional fundamentalist denomination being the true indigenous form of spirituality in our area (e.g., Southern Baptist, Methodist, Church of Christ, etc.). I also knew by now that my family had been Baptist before they became Jehovah's Witness, and so I felt a type of ancestral duty to embrace something similar. Against these points, though, were two others: one, that all these legacy denominations seemed to be physically dying (no new members) and suffocatingly inconsequential in the grand scheme of things. And two, I kept having, as I said, this irresistible attraction to Roman Catholicism. Part of it was purely aesthetic: I could see that statues and images and colors and sounds and smells and rituals were integral parts of all the ancient, venerable religions, such as Buddhism, Hinduism, and most forms of paganism, and Catholicism seemed like the closest thing to a home team version of one of those.

The historically accurate thing to have done would have been to stick it out with the blue-haired Baptists while the socially and politically advantageous thing would have been to join a rip-roaring megachurch. The former seemed anticlimactic, and the latter seemed completely unappealing. Personally, I do not think worship should be conducted with guitars, drums, and a killer hook. This was something Plato worked out 2,500 years ago in the *Republic*: certain musical meters produce predictable effects in the human psyche.[1] There's a reason why gangster rap and club music sound the way they do: those beats and rhythms are designed to get you in an aggressive or sexual mood. Imagine Lil Wayne's "(I Wish I could (expletive)) Every Girl in the World" set to the tune of "Highland Cathedral." What you get is no longer an aphrodisiac but a joke. Conversely, taking "A Thousand

---

1. Pl. *Rep.* 3.398d–399c, translated by Grube and Reeve.

Miles" by Vanessa Carlton and addressing it to Jesus in no way absolves it of its mawkishness. Pop is pop, mom rock is mom rock, and heavy metal is heavy metal—they're designed to make you feel the way they do, and even if they can be catchy or interesting, or even moving in some cases, they're lacking as guides to the heights of spiritual experience.

Different strokes for different folks, many will say. Just let them have their form of worship while you have yours! That sounds great and accords perfectly with our relativistic, consumerist society, but that's not how *man* works. That's not how the physics of music works. And not acknowledging this is what has led to the loss of the sacred in our churches and society.

What's funny is that the Catholic Church I started visiting during this time had anything but a beautiful, traditional liturgy. But coming as I did from the most puritanical, iconoclastic Protestant sect ever conceived, where we didn't even put up crosses and where hymns were pre-recorded piano riffs we sang over top of, I guess my standards were pretty low. Just the fact of a liturgical structure at all struck something deep and primal within me. After hitting up a few Sunday masses, I impulsively decided I would join the RCIA (Rite of Christian Initiation for Adults) class.

That sounds drastic—I go from thinking maybe church is politically or socially beneficial to contemplating joining the Roman Catholic Church? But again, it's not that I accepted the Church's or even Christ's claims. I had read that monastic book by Merton, nodding approvingly when he talked about quiet and interior peace and grimacing when he started on about the Holy Trinity and the Virgin Mary. If I was going to join a church, though, I realized I wouldn't be satisfied unless I joined the Catholic one, despite all the good reasons not to. If I had had any idea of what that entailed, I wouldn't have considered it. But being essentially a liberal perennialist by this point, I figured, why not?

And I'm disappointed to report that RCIA didn't do much to disabuse me of that notion. The people were very kind and welcoming, but the instruction wasn't much more than a how-to on Catholic distinctives, like holy water and the sign of the cross. They must've said in there somewhere that the Catholic Church says certain things are true and "thou shalt believe them," and other things are bad and "thou shalt not do them," but I didn't hear it. Either through a lack of emphasis on their part or just an unwillingness (or unreadiness) to hear on my part, I came away in basically the same intellectual position vis-à-vis the Church as when I started; namely, that this is a beautiful, ancient, and beneficial way of life but in the end still just one way among many with no special claims to my allegiance.

However, even as I grew in the knowledge of God through RCIA, my feet were hastening ever more quickly to badness in my personal life. It was my junior year of college, and my sterling academic record looked to be in trouble: weekends were increasingly occupied with benders and copious amounts of recovery time rather than paper writing. I'd discovered that work stood to benefit too from a little pre-shift imbibing. Who didn't enjoy a looser, more sociable customer service rep? Granted, this involved me driving under the influence in order to get to work with a fresh buzz, but that was a risk I felt was justified. It may shock and horrify you to know that most drunk drivers have driven intoxicated hundreds of times before they finally get caught or cause an accident. Sadly, it was important enough to me that I feel comfortable and confident and that other people see a particular version of me that the potential for a DUI or, what's worse, seriously injuring or killing someone seemed like an acceptable trade-off. The level of self-absorption is staggering. And yet, that's what alcoholism is: stupid, backward, self-serving priorities completely divorced from reality.

It was early in the second semester that things finally came to a head, and a new day dawned after the deepest darkness. My wife had left for an extended stay with her parents, and it was left up in the air as to whether she would return or not. You might think this would've distressed me, but by this point I welcomed the extra drinking time: now it would come with less nagging. Having the boys up to the newly consequence-free joint house became my main priority in life. It was usually Levi, along with one or two others. And my always-down-to-party neighbors would definitely be up for it.

After one particularly raucous session, I was at my post at the customer service desk at the Kroger on Charlotte Pike. I had transferred to this location after moving to Nashville. At that time it was a working-class grocery store serving, among other West Nashville neighborhoods, the Nations, where I had some roots (my great-aunt and -uncle rolled in on the motorized buggies every so often). It was about even in population between blacks and whites, with a smattering of immigrants. I felt a kindred spirit with these people and had settled in nicely (if raging alcoholics can be said to settle). That particular night I was feeling the effects of the previous night's activities. I was bleary-eyed and queasy. My head was pounding. I was sure no one else noticed the state I was in. I had, though, quietly admitted to a coworker in my torpidity that I needed to go to Alcoholics Anonymous (AA). I didn't know anything about AA, only that, from the sound of it, it must be for people like me.

A few minutes later, a smallish man with glasses and a goatee stopped by the customer service desk and said, "I heard you mention AA when I first came in. My name's Eric, and here's my phone number, if you'd like to know more or to come check it out sometime."

My eyes widened. I think I managed an awkward, "Thank you," as I took the scrap of paper with his number on it. I stood staring at it for a few seconds and then hastily excused myself.

I emerged into the cold January night air of that Kroger parking lot and felt my eyes welling up. In an instant, my entire philosophy of life—God, religion, the nature of reality—came crashing down into the sand upon which it was built. The thundercloud of God's presence engulfed me. I sensed it, all at once: purposeful, providential care; loving pursuit of the lost; the unmistakable communication to my withered and corrupted mind of everything I'd never dared to believe. I turned to the on-duty policeman hired for security: "God is real! He sent someone to tell me about AA! I had just been telling someone I needed to go, and then this man just walks up and gives me his number!"

"I think God," he said, "is trying to tell you something. Better listen."

Maybe that all sounds ridiculous to you, if you're an atheist or a nonbeliever. I understand that these "extremely unlikely coincidence" proofs for God's existence seem like sentimental claptrap to people not directly involved. But here's the thing: it's not meant to convince *you*: it was meant to convince *me*. Consider: if God is who he says he is, either he could wind up the universe from the foundation of the world to run on its own principles until his purpose is accomplished, or he could "poof" the desired effect into existence from outside the system. The second method is what we usually restrict the word *miracle* to, probably to satisfy the skeptics. But the first, for those affected by it, is no less personally miraculous and undeniable. My experience was undoubtedly of that first variety: I know for a fact that Eric wasn't magically transported to my desk to give me that message, but the events unfolded with such perfect precision and carried such monumental significance for my life that I can only conclude that they were intentional purposes on the part of an omniscient Mind.

I owe this line of thinking to Peter Kreeft,[2] but follow me: if there's a God who prizes our freedom and wants us to choose to love him, then to blind each and every one of us with spectacular miracles would spoil the "free" aspect of that choice. If he could instead use demonstrations of his loving concern and power that are just convincing enough to those who are open to him but that could still plausibly be rejected by those who stubbornly insist on denying him, wouldn't it make sense that such "subtle" interventions would be the normal way in which he would reveal himself? In certain cases, he does "blind," so to speak, mortals with proof of his existence (at the Resurrection of Christ, for instance, or Fatima's dance of the sun, or one of the innumerable miraculous healings accomplished by saintly intercession). But in general, the proof comes in this way: it's undeniable to those who are looking, and unconvincing to those who aren't or won't. And at a certain level of obstinacy, not even miracles work (like with the ancient Israelites after their deliverance from Egypt).

The point is that now everything in my life was different. This God, whoever or whatever he was, was looking out for me—seeking me, even. God had gone from an improbable but nice theory, to a reality bigger than any I'd ever encountered. What would I do with this? Well, I took Eric up on his offer and met him at an AA meeting. I got the literature, sat through the meeting, and discussed my situation with him. "You have all the telltale signs of being an alcoholic," he told me.

I could logically see that. I saw that if I started to drink, I would inevitably get drunk. With each passing drink the will to resist the next one diminished. I saw that, like an alcoholic, I had tried to implement schemes to prevent blackouts, such as staying away from hard liquor or never drinking alone (both of which failed). And I saw that every bloodshot next-morning oath I'd taken I'd broken, no matter how sincere it felt. I saw all this, and yet as if to prove my point about obstinacy in the face of miracles, I told Eric after a couple of meetings, "Thanks for the info. I think this knowledge was what I needed to get my drinking under control." He just shook his head and smiled.

I can't remember what occasioned the binge to end all binges, but a couple weeks after my brush with AA, the boys and I went on a tear like no other. It started on a Wednesday evening. We toured many of the other units in the apartment building, carrying on late into the night, disturbing any and everyone. Next day we woke up late and sought to avoid our

---

2. Kreeft, *Fundamentals*, 44–45.

impending fate by turning to the hair of the dog. The only problem was that I had to work that afternoon. In short order, however, I was much too drunk for that. I had called out of work a few times prior to this in order to drink, and so when I dialed up work and told them I was sick again, they were understandably unamused. It was a tense conversation with the assistant manager, whose voice gave away that he knew something. I maintained my story and hung up with a mixture of relief and anger. Who were they to be so pushy about me missing one stupid little shift? It was true I didn't feel good! Well, never mind that: I now had 24 more hours of freedom.

The empty cases of beer would eventually pile six feet high in my living room. A shady friend of mine from college joined us that night as well. As we began to lose steam after a solid day's drinking, he offered us a way to extend the magic. Despite the awesome *Pulp Fiction*-esque nosebleed, I passed out after a while, and the others were left to their own devices, making manic phone calls and lighting cigarettes off the stove.

I awoke the next bright morning to impenetrable darkness. My senses were bombarded by the smoldering wreckage all around me. My eyes surveyed the detritus of beer cases, cans, and stains. My nose took in the lingering layers of caked-on cigarette smoke and the putrid staleness of discarded butts. My ears reverberated with the pounding in my head and the snoring of the catatonic carousers. And my soul was submerged in a filthy morass of shame, grief, guilt, and regret. What had I done? Even with the parts I could remember, that question remained (to say nothing of all the patches of oblivion I'd drifted in and out of). I'd brazenly lied and put everyone at work in a bind. I'd ravaged my body with something like 48 beers in even fewer hours, to say nothing of the multiple packs' worth of cigarettes and other things. And I'd surely pissed off some neighbors (or several), who would probably be telling on me to the landlord.

Everyone woke up and slowly stumbled out the door. The party was over. That's always a letdown, but this time it was more profound. I didn't want it to be over, but I was also sick of it. It was like someone else, some demon, had come and done this and left me holding the bag at the end of it all. And what was waiting for me at work? Surely hell. I was going in that afternoon.

Somehow later that morning I ended up at my grandma's house over on Colorado Avenue. She was being put in a home, and we were selling the house to pay for it. From the front yard I dialed Eric.

"I got drunk for two straight days, ravaged my body, and lied to my boss. I do need AA; I can't live like this."

I could visualize his smile. "Good," he said. "Well, meet me at the clubhouse tomorrow at noon. And you'll have to tell your boss what you did."

"Shoot, I guess you're right," I said. But I was somehow relieved.

I got to work earlier that afternoon. I had called ahead and told them I needed to tell them something. I walked into the store manager's office.

"I wanted to tell you that I lied the other day. I wasn't sick—I was getting drunk and partying." My voice cracked. "But I want you to know that I've got someone helping me now and I'm going to AA tomorrow to quit drinking."

"We figured you were lying," she said. "We've actually had several complaints at different times from customers saying you smelled like alcohol. We'd been trying to catch you but just hadn't been able to yet."

My eyes got big. I had no idea! But I always chewed gum and ate pungent things to cover the smell! How did anyone know?

She continued: "We'll give you one more shot, if you're serious. I don't want to have to fire you, but believe me, I will, if this type of behavior doesn't stop."

I could tell she wanted to see me get better, though. I thanked her earnestly and went back up front and started my shift.

Chapter 6

The Outlines of Reality

A feeling of wholesome humility radiated from every fiber of my being that night. I had been a sorry excuse for a man, and I was sorry about it. I had been given a new lease on life. But behind the quiet gratitude was a distressing question. If I had gone back to my old ways so soon after God had broken into my life so dramatically, all current happy feelings aside, what if I really couldn't stop? I had been sure of God's desire to save me from myself, and yet even that didn't stop the worst eruption of that same self. What if I wasn't strong (or sane) enough to overcome this darkness?

Well, I wasn't, but that was the point, as I would soon learn. Not only did I start going to an AA meeting every day, I also immediately asked Eric to be my sponsor. Shaken to my core, I put myself totally under his direction. A sponsor in AA is someone who has gone through the twelve steps of recovery and maintains active sobriety, which means not drinking, of course, but also going to meetings and doing service for others. Eric had something like ten years of sobriety then and was very involved. I couldn't have been given a better guide. Every spiritual director or counselor I've had since has paled in comparison.

I often say that I'm lucky my major malfunction is alcoholism and not something less blatantly destructive, like food or video game addiction. Alcoholism is such a clear and present danger, universally condemned by society, that there are more resources available for sufferers and a public awareness of what getting better looks like and requires. No doubt this is due to the notoriety of AA. If it weren't for my very public alcoholism, I would've never embarked upon the intensive program of emotional maturation required by AA. In part it's just basic growing up. It's said that an alcoholic's level of maturity freezes at the age when he first starts drinking. This is because alcohol's numbing effects take the place of processing emotions and integrating the personality with reality. Reality is not faced and assimilated but avoided. So, as a twenty-year-old, I basically had the maturity level of a sixteen- or seventeen-year-old. I think that fact is amply borne out by the narrative up to this point.

Eric had me working through the steps with writing assignments each night, and we talked on the phone every day. He convinced me (and it took very little convincing) that my life was unmanageable, and that as it stood, I *could not* stop drinking on my own power, even if I wanted to. But he and AA claimed that there was a "higher power," called God by many, who could and indeed would "restore me to sanity" if I could manage to have a spiritual awakening. The twelve steps were the how-to of this awakening.

There are some very scary parts to the whole process: turning your will and your life over to the care of this higher power; performing "a searching and fearless moral inventory" of your entire life, and then confessing it to another person; making amends to everyone you've ever hurt, when possible and prudent. There's a very practical reason these steps result in a spiritual awakening, apart from any action of the divine—they're a dramatically new way of living, not only for alcoholics, but for most people. It's a way of life anchored in humble honesty. All pretenses must be dropped; all reservations released; any crutch clung to flung away. If you've never experienced the state of total honesty with yourself, God, and another human being, I can only say that it is life changing. It's the type of thing that's only possible, though, for those desperate enough to trust their fate to the Living God. The reality of such a God is the only ontological basis which could justify such a radically vulnerable posture. Conceive, if you will, of the beauty of being so free, so unburdened with solicitude for yourself, that you could approach those you've wronged—wronged deeply in many cases—boldly acknowledge exactly what evil you've done, and expect no reciprocation; expect nothing, really—your only aim being the setting right of things to whatever degree possible. Imagine being convinced that your own survival depended on serving others—that now it wasn't just something commendable to do, but something essential to your new way of life. This is the radicalism that only the dying can have.

I came to this realization slowly, but AA is essentially just Christianity stripped of the proper names. And the spiritual awakening it brings about is one of the surest proofs of God's existence that I could imagine. I had already come around on that question based on my initial encounter at the customer service desk, but working the twelve steps showed his presence to me unmistakably and gave me the practical tools for living according to this belief.

Alcoholics can't just *stop drinking*. As I said earlier, we're born with a bottle-shaped hole, a slot that says, "insert alcohol here." Alcohol was the solution before it was the problem. It *fixed* me—it just also caused all kinds of unwanted side effects. To ask me to quit was to ask me to choose between two sets of problems: the seemingly superficial alcohol-caused ones that until recently had seemed manageable—and the primordial problem of *me*.

AA didn't ask me to pick between those two, though. It offered me a remedy that promised to fix the original problem but with no harmful side effects, if I was brave (or desperate) enough to try it. It seemed improbable, even impossible, that it could work. But by the grace of God, over thirteen years later, I'm still sober. The last time I seriously wanted a drink was six months into sobriety. I think I hadn't quite finished the steps yet, and, feeling good about how much my life had improved lately, I took a notion that a celebratory beer might be in order. I mean, alcohol is essential to life and culture, right? I didn't want to live like a puritan forever, so certainly with all the knowledge and experience I'd gained in AA, I ought to be able to enjoy a drink now and then like an adult, right? And thus the madness began...

AA had sunk in enough though that I had the innocence to call my sponsor and inform him of what I planned to do. "I think I'm ready for a drink," I said confidently. "I think I've earned it. Why can't I just have a beer or two?"

"Okay," Eric said calmly. "Do me a favor, though. Don't do it tonight. Pray about it tonight; then, if you feel the same way in the morning, go ahead."

Sure, I can do that, I chuckled to myself. I wasn't living like an addict anymore, so waiting a day shouldn't be any skin off my back.

I did as instructed—prayed, didn't drink, and went to bed—fully intending to crack one open on the morrow. I awoke the next day with no desire to drink, and let me tell you—I've never been seriously tempted like that again, God be praised. Sometimes, all he needs from us is the tiniest bit of willingness and trust. If it's his will, he can move mountains with even that.

So on February 14, 2010, I resumed growing up. And there were many growing pains. I realized my marriage had been contracted for all the wrong reasons. She did come home that summer, but we were soon separated again, this time for good. Before then, though, I had another decision to make. Remember that I had been in the RCIA class this whole time, moving steadily toward Easter, when we were to decide whether we wanted to enter the church or not. Despite the fact that I now believed in a personal God, I did not believe that he was actually the father of Jesus Christ in any true or literal sense. I still believed that all religions were basically the same thing. And yet, when Easter came, I chose to become Catholic. It was because of that same strange pull it had always exercised on me. I figured, if I'm going to have a religion, it might as well be this one, one I at least kind of like. And so on April 3, 2010, I received baptism, confirmation, and Holy Eucharist at the hands of Father Phillip Breen (of happy memory) at St. Ann's in West Nashville and became a Christian.

It wasn't long, though, before I was chasing the Protestant idea again, seeking to appease both my vague religious leanings and my political, social, and cultural hang-ups at the same time. I fell off going to Mass and started researching Protestant denominations from a historical and cultural perspective again. But I repeatedly ran up against the same problem: if I found one that particularly satisfied me, it was inevitably too small and irrelevant to feel serious, and it certainly wasn't an expression of any local, rooted cultural ethos.

I entered senior year, newly single and back on my feet academically. I applied for and got accepted to do my final semester in our nation's capital through the Washington Center. They matched me up with the National Trust for Historic Preservation, where I would be interning and writing for their Main Street Division. They put me up in a condo tower on the edge of Old Town Alexandria, within walking distance of the Blue and Orange Metro lines. I roomed with one fellow from Massachusetts and another from Seoul, South Korea.

I felt like I was being ushered into the professional class with the experience: there were "networking events" and workshops for developing your "power greeting" and refining your self-promotional "elevator sales pitch." We were even given a personal interview with our Congressman. We were also wined and dined somewhat, with free tours of places like the U.S. Capitol building. I greatly enjoyed this latte lifestyle: riding the packed trains during the morning rush hour, sampling the endless cultural offerings of the District, and cavorting in packed, sweaty nightclubs on the weekends.

I didn't let any of the worldly delights stop me from jumping immediately into the DC/Northern Virginia AA scene, which I discovered to be alive with a similar demographic and energy. I made a point to get involved and volunteer, and I benefited richly from it in the friends and memories I made. The bond of AA kept everyone hungry to help out, and our many sober parties and events (like a city-wide scavenger hunt that was riotous fun) further increased our fellow feeling. In general, I was also starting to appreciate not only my present life but the world and its history. The imposing monuments, parks, and public buildings all impressed upon me the grandeur of the nation they represented. They were more than the sum total of their parts: they sacralized what they portrayed, solidifying those mystic chords of memory I had begun to perceive. My experience of patriotism began here and has only grown since. It's partly why I think today's "woke" iconoclasm is one of the greatest threats facing the West. It's not that by erecting or leaving up a monument of a historical figure that we're condoning every single thing he did. Not even saints come with that guarantee in the Catholic Church. What we're saying is that this person did *something* admirable, and that his life is an integral part of the collective story. And just because that story now actively includes people and groups that were formerly excluded does not give us the right to erase what that monument meant to our forefathers and what they intended it to mean for us.

The point of patriotism is the lived experience of the collective story, the finding of oneself in that broad and deep stream. I love the story of America, even if, for instance, it's plagued with anti-Catholicism. I bracket that and try to appreciate either the partial notions of the good that were behind such actions, or I choose to emphasize more congenial parts. I say again, I love my country's history. It's part of me and I'm part of it. It colors and brings meaning to the most nondescript knoll or ramshackle shack. Someone who talks about loving this country while wanting to consign its heroes to a museum doesn't love this country at all—he loves an idea. No matter how loudly some might insist that America is nothing more than an "ideal," or a "propositional nation," there are bones in our hallowed hills that ceaselessly refute them.

That semester had another singularly profound effect on me that has lasted to this day, and God willing will perdure to eternity. At an AA house party somewhere in Northern Virginia, I met Rosalyn, who I found out was a Christian after a few minutes of conversation. I was calling myself a Christian at this point, but more as a cultural identifier (something that fit being a Tennessean, I thought). Somehow she ended up giving me the book *More Than a Carpenter* by Josh and Sean McDowell. I don't even remember why—did it come up that I didn't truly believe, or did she just sense that and tell me to read the book? Whatever the case, I took the book and agreed to read it.

I can imagine many skeptics, or even some of the more sophisticated Catholics, turning their noses up at such pop apologetics as *More Than a Carpenter*.[1] All I can say is that with each passing page of the book, the realization dawned on me: "This stuff could actually be true." Christianity, as this book and others such as *The Case for Christ* by Lee Strobel and *Fundamentals of the Faith* by Peter Kreeft illustrate, is different from all other religions. It is the only religion based on a publicly attested miracle and spread by multiple eyewitnesses. Buddhism, for all its admirable qualities, is more a method for achieving a type of peace than a definite claim about the supernatural realm. Hinduism and most forms of paganism are personifications of nature with implicit ethical systems. There isn't some great proof they produce in asking for your belief: they merely draw your attention to the way the world is and explain it, usually in a poetic and beautiful way. Islam is a religious and political system delivered to one man privately, who then spread it to others. It is an exaltation of a great new prophet whose claim to be speaking for God we must accept on faith.

But Christianity is different. Christianity's holy writ was not written centuries after the events contained in them. As *More Than a Carpenter* shows, some of Paul's letters can be dated to the 50s AD—that's only twenty years after the miracles and resurrection of Christ were supposed to have occurred. And many estimates of the Gospels themselves date them to the decades immediately following. If I were to tell you that, twenty years ago, I had seen someone killed in the most brutal manner, and that this man came back to life three days later and was seen by more than five hundred people, many of whom are still alive; and further, that the whole social movement I've given my life to hinges on this fact—what would you think? What if I then accepted a life of privation and hardship because I wouldn't stop promoting this unbelievable story, and was eventually killed for it?

Well, that's exactly what St. Paul does in the first letter to the Corinthian church (15:3–8). Many scholars, including atheist and nonbelieving

---

1. I've also become cognizant of deeper, more paradigmatic proofs for Christianity in recent years, but I still maintain that the "evidentialist" route to faith I initially took is helpful.

ones, date the "creedal statement" there to the thirties AD—mere years after the events they purport to describe. We are dealing here, then, not with fantastical myths written down centuries after the alleged events, but with either hundreds of delusional lunatics and pathological liars, or with hundreds of sincerely convinced eyewitnesses. Given their persistence under intense persecution, which scenario seems most likely?

And all this was put to scrutiny. The Jewish leaders in Jerusalem were trying desperately to quash the nascent movement. Every trick was surely tried to discredit the Apostles. If it were all a lie, it would've been pretty easily disproved. Paul refers to the witnesses of the risen Jesus in a way that implies, "And you can go ask them if you don't believe me." He says of them: "Most of [them] are still living, though some have fallen asleep" (1 Corinthians 15:6). Surely some hard-nosed sleuth of the first century could've left us the record (or the result, which might've looked like the fizzling out of the movement) of this epic "fact check" wherein he debunked all of Paul's claims: don't forget, power and money were backing up *that* position, not the young Christian church. Every resource would've been at the disposal of someone doing such an exposé. And yet the historical record is silent. Of all Paul's diatribes, the one against "the rationalizers who attempted to discredit my witnesses" is nowhere to be found. Certainly we would have some trace of a polemical literature between Christians and their enemies citing dueling witnesses, each accusing the other of having threatened and/or bribed to extract the desired testimony. But beyond the initial weak claim by the authorities in Jerusalem that the Apostles took the body, we hear of no serious refutation gaining currency. Instead, just brute repression, which many times is the last resort of people who've lost an argument.

I'm sure you can find the odd scholar who says that Paul's creed and letters don't date from those early times, but at a certain point we're just playing scholars like Pokémon cards. You can find a study that proves anything. The fact that a majority of scholars believe in the early dating doesn't prove it beyond a shadow of a doubt either, but it is a good clue. That's all any of this is: induction, or little bits of a larger case. When I view the actions of the early Christians, it looks more to me like they were sincere and telling the truth than the alternative. Lies and myths can spread and be believed sincerely, but not when the claim is so falsifiable, and not when those in power are working to expose it as if their societal position depended on it (it did).

The early Christians were revealing that the deepest longing of the heart—that death should be conquered—had come true, and to prove it to you they sealed their testimony in blood. Do purveyors of today's conspiracy theories put forth scores of living witnesses? Do they ever accept *death* rather than renounce their absurd claims? Sure, people like to talk, but how many people could be made to testify under oath that the moon landing was faked, much less under penalty of death?

It staggers belief to maintain that the whole thing could be one big hermetically sealed hoax. And that's why it spread like wildfire in the Mediterranean world with no institutional backing: its argument was sincerity. There were tons of weird cults at the time, many with similar ceremonies (Mithraism, for example). None had the same force of conviction and power that Christianity did because they were theories, not testimonies.

C.S. Lewis explicated a lot of this half a century ago with his "Lord, Liar, or Lunatic" trilemma.[2] He showed how the idea that Christ was just a wise guru is a nonsensical position. Moderns thought they had found a way out of the trilemma by making it into a quadrilemma: they added "myth" as a fourth option. But it's apologists like the McDowells, Kreeft, and Strobel (using modern New Testament scholarship) who have exploded this theory. One such scholar who has acted on his findings that the Resurrection is credible is N.T. Wright, a bishop in the Church of England. I refer you to him for the full scholarly treatment.[3]

I continued to read these other writers as time went on, but it was clear to me after *More Than a Carpenter* where the evidence pointed. This God that had reached in and saved me from alcoholic destruction was none other than the father of Jesus Christ, who had lived, died, and risen from the grave nearly 2,000 years ago. Other faiths didn't even try to make the same kind of case for themselves that Christianity did. Christianity, then, wasn't just a nice, culturally appropriate skin suit for my vague spiritual leanings: it was a vitally important concern with potentially life or death consequences.

I took a deep dive immediately into Protestant theology. The old Catholic yearning was still lurking, and I needed to understand what the substantive issues of disagreement were. If Christ is risen, there must be some way in which we can worship him today—there must be some "correct" denomination, I reasoned. Maybe you question that. Maybe you believe in

---

2. Lewis, *Mere Christianity*, 52
3. Wright, *Resurrection*.

him and yet think everyone else is getting it wrong, and so no one's under any obligation to join a church. I disagree for the following reasons. Both Old and New Testament religion was communal, which meant that there was a tangible, physical community one had to belong to. Also, it doesn't fit with the way the God of the Bible did things. He always had a representative or channel, as the JWs would say, in the real world—he never left his people orphans. The answer, then, had to be among the options his providence had allowed to exist here and now. Otherwise I might as well make up my own idiosyncratic blend of Christianity and call it a day.

I settled on *sola fide*, or salvation by faith alone, as being the fault line between Catholicism and Protestantism. Many astute Protestant apologists have done similarly, illustrating this point in the "Jesus > religion" meme that was floating around at the time. The idea is that "Christianity" (i.e., Protestantism) is the only religion on the planet that says your works and efforts are completely useless. You're saved by *faith* and not by works—it's God's grace alone that saves you, and therefore, unlike all other religions, Christianity is the only one that frees man from works-based righteousness, which means reliance on self rather than God. This struck a chord with me because it seemed like a real distinctive, another hard dividing line that made a difference. As I read Paul's letters, the doctrine seemed to jump out at me. It was about faith, not "works of the law" (Romans 3:20).

"Here I stand: I can do naught else." Martin Luther's immortal words on the subject seemed fitting now to me. This was the authentic Gospel that the Reformers had recovered, and it placed Protestant Christianity on one side of a dividing line and every other religion (including Catholicism) on the other. It didn't matter if Catholicism had smells and bells and beauty: *this* was the Gospel. Here I must stand.

But, alas, even settling upon Evangelicalism brings you to the doorstep of another dilemma: Calvinism or Arminianism? Calvinism is pretty notorious—it comes with the idea of double predestination (God sets aside so many people for Heaven and so many people for Hell from the foundation of the world) and basically lays out a five-point system that is nothing more than the logical consequence of sola fide and *sola gratia* (salvation by grace alone). Arminians (named after Jacobus Arminius, a Dutch theologian) are much more numerous but lesser known because most of them don't call themselves that. They nominally accept Calvin's five points but fudge them a bit to avoid admitting double predestination, thus preserving some notion of free will. The debate between the two camps is evidenced by Baptist Church factions in the South. The Primitive Baptists represent those Baptists who were so committed to predestination that they stopped doing missions and evangelizing. Why bother if God's totally in control? In reaction, the Free Will Baptists were formed. They were so convinced of the need for evangelization and of double predestination's incompatibility with such a call that they rejected parts of Calvinism in favor of an explicit formulation of man's free will as crucial to salvation.

I saw immediately that Calvinism was pretty unpopular in the major evangelical denominations. It's ascendant only with the more self-selecting, highly educated, upwardly mobile groups. There's the Presbyterian Church in America, as well as certain Dutch Reformed and covenantal Baptist denominations. These groups are fairly marginal. The most hopeful sign for Calvinists is their growth within certain prominent Southern Baptist Convention (SBC) congregations, which somehow culminated in Dr. R. Albert Mohler, a leading Calvinist theologian, being placed as the head of the denomination's seminary in Louisville. The SBC never took a stand either way on the status of Calvinism within the denomination. Calvinists can point to several of the group's most prolific spokesmen of the nineteenth century as being of their number.

One of those influential Calvinist congregations happened to be located in Washington, DC: Capitol Hill Baptist Church, pastored by Mark Dever. The crowd there was young, educated, and affluent (like most of DC these days), and the church had everything this demographic could want: a historic church building; copious use of traditional hymns (albeit mixed in with newer ones, perhaps to appear less stuffy); and a specific, intellectually rigorous theology firmly rooted in the Reformed tradition. I was intrigued. I made contacts my first time attending and set up some lunch dates.

I was also getting hooked on their theological texts. There's something embodied and rooted in adopting a specific religious tradition that includes what you could call "totems": statements of faith and catechisms, as well as the writings of great men who lived at a particular place and time. People want to feel like they're part of something larger, some august chain of transmission. The problem is that modern culture is set up to kill this instinct at all costs. Most people therefore stumble about unknowingly and unconsciously forget this impulse. An intellectual's problem is that he thinks too deeply and inwardly to forget it for too long. He needs some basis to stand upon; otherwise he's too self-conscious of his shallow roots to go forward with confidence in life.

But there's an irony in rallying under the standard of something like Calvinism. Calvinism, and Protestantism generally, is premised on the ruthless critique of theological tradition. To then turn such a system into a crystallized test of orthodoxy and effectively canonize its historic proponents is a capricious and contradictory move.

Calvinism as an identity with a storied tradition, as a "given," is anti-Calvinist. But it's as human as it gets. Remembering, memorializing, mythologizing—these are how man naturally treats the sacred, the meaningful, the eternal. In its rejection of these, Calvinism shows itself to be a species of liberalism and the (proto) Enlightenment project to remake society along "rational" lines. Because of its rationalist origin, the essence of Protestantism resists being sacralized in this "superstitious" way, and so the mass of semi-Calvinist Christians out there who have no knowledge of Calvin or the Westminster Confession of Faith are being more consistent than the intellectuals attempting to enshrine their confessional past. Paradoxically, then, the Calvinist-descended nondenominational movement at the forefront of Evangelicalism (which wants nothing to do with Calvin) is Calvin's truest heir. Every generation must invent the faith anew—jettison the old hymns, forget the archaic divines and their dusty tomes, tear down the old sanctuary and raise up a "worship auditorium"—this is what it means to be truly "Reformed."

But I wasn't cognizant of all that. In my meetings with the reformers, someone gave me some John Stott booklets when I mentioned not being "saved" yet. For most Evangelicals, getting saved is the way one actually becomes a Christian. My Catholic baptism hadn't "done" anything in that department according to them. I read the Stott booklets.[4] They were well-written little treatises, classier than the standard fare you get in this department—I'm thinking of those tracts with the flames of Hell on the front. It gave simple instructions for getting saved, including a prayer.

I felt as though I had come to another precipice and was being asked to jump again. God was real. He'd saved me from alcoholism. I was convinced this God I'd encountered was the same one the Israelites had approached with fear and trembling several thousand years before. And now I felt that despite the aesthetic appeal of Catholicism, Protestantism preserved the pure Gospel and represented the worship of this God in spirit and truth. All that was left, according to these Baptists, was to say this simple prayer and mean it, and Heaven could be mine. I knelt down in the room I shared with

4. Stott, *Becoming a Christian*.

my roommate (he wasn't present), and began: "Lord Jesus Christ, I *humbly acknowledge* that I have sinned in my thinking and speaking and acting, that I am guilty of deliberate wrongdoing. . ." and so forth, ending with, "Come in, Lord Jesus, and be my Savior and my Lord for ever. Amen."[5]

I opened my eyes and felt a lightness like I'd never felt before. The room looked different to me. I stood up and felt a rush of gratitude. I was saved. I belonged to Christ now. A wonderful transaction had taken place, and it felt like beams of light were emanating from my face. I immediately told my roommates. The one from Massachusetts expressed surprise that I hadn't already been saved (I guess he assumed most Southerners were). I told almost everyone over the next few days.

My euphoria genuinely lasted two to three days and helped convince me that I had made the right choice going with Evangelicalism. Before this I'd nearly settled on staying Catholic a few times, though I felt weird now about the way I'd come in. Why had I gone ahead with Catholic baptism when I hadn't really believed in it? I'd taken the red line out to the Catholic University of America several times because of a nagging desire to be present at Mass that I couldn't shake. I even went to confession a few times in order to receive Communion (was it the actual Body of Christ?). I learned in the confessional a good deal more about sin than I'd been taught in RCIA. I couldn't deny the tractor beam pull that the Mass had on me. Did it just happen to tickle my fancy? I shared this with one of my new Reformed friends.

"I've had this attraction to the Catholic Church that's hard to shake. I think maybe just because it seems so Tolkien-esque—like it seems like a fairy tale, with its holy water and sacraments and pilgrimages and whatnot."

"Yeah," he said uneasily, "they've got that market cornered." He seemed either uncomfortable, or worried that I was. We both agreed that extraneous stuff like that didn't matter, though. What was important were the Doctrines of Grace, and avoiding idol worship.

To bolster my resolve as the fuzzy feelings faded, I ordered and read Abraham Kuyper's *Lectures on Calvinism*. Kuyper was a Dutch theologian and one of the greatest minds to put pen to paper in the Reformed tradition. He mounts a brilliant defense of Calvinism and even states that, within Christianity, there are only two poles; two complete, self-subsistent systems: Calvinism and Catholicism. All other flavors are varying amalgams of these two. He also is at pains to demonstrate that, far from being culture-denying or primitive, the Calvinist rejection of images in worship evinces the height

---

5. Stott, *Becoming a Christian*.

of culture. Using a somewhat Platonic lens, he posits that all things purely rational and abstract are higher than the visible and tangible. Primitive religion needs helps and totems and the sensible. The highest, purest form of worship, on the other hand, dispenses with these. I was very impressed with this line of reasoning, and it removed my explicit reservations.

A few factors kept me from settling into Calvinism, however. One was the question of whether it was absolutely necessary. Back home, what if I couldn't find a Reformed Baptist Church? I wanted to be Baptist—it both made the most sense to me and was the church of my family before JWism. It would be more socially advantageous, all things being equal, to be a regular old Arminian Baptist. Second, the Reformed elders were telling me I needed to go back to my ex-wife. Couldn't they see that whole debacle never should've happened in the first place? I knew Catholics had the idea of annulment—that seemed like a fit for my situation, though I'm sure I was quite biased in the matter.

I decided to check out a mainstream Southern Baptist Church before committing myself at Capitol Hill Baptist. I showed up one Sunday at Downtown Baptist Church in Alexandria. I was immediately presented with a more familiar picture: church ladies, sanctuary carpet, and Southern accents. I asked if I could help clean up after the service, and before I knew it I had met the pastor and set up a lunch date. When we met I told him my story. He was fascinated, and after a few more meetings he asked if I would respond to the altar call (even though I'd already been saved—he said to think of it as a dramatic reenactment for the crowd) and submit to a re-baptism—the Catholic one didn't count because it wasn't full immersion, and because it had preceded, rather than followed, my acceptance of Christ as Lord and Savior. It sounds more suspect than it was; he wasn't an opportunist or showman in any way. The story just needed the proper *presentation* or it wouldn't be as well-received. He also wanted me to take to the mic and say a few words afterwards.

These Baptists were generous, kind people, and many promises were made to stay in touch after I went back to Tennessee that were sadly never kept. When time came to go home for graduation, I had dozens of heartfelt goodbyes to say, between my church family, my AA community, and my Washington Center peers. I had come to DC/NOVA with a hunger for life and, thanks to my AA training from Eric, the discipline to go after it. I had been taught to make myself useful, to put myself out there, even when fear, anxiety, or sloth told me I shouldn't, and the results were beyond my wildest dreams. I had found community and belonging in three short months, even if I would never see most of them ever again. It was an instructive lesson: wherever you are, no matter how short your time there, put down roots. That place, that time, those people—they're worth it.

I got back to Tennessee and graduated college, the first to do so in my family, with my degree in urban studies. But this was 2011, and the downturn from the Great Recession hadn't quite ended yet. It seemed that I really had no marketable skills. I had done a lot with geographic information systems (GIS), but not enough to have a certificate, and not to the extent that I could confidently convince anyone that I knew how to use it. I moved back in with my parents; they agreed to a short stay since I was clean now. I commenced going to AA meetings and hanging out with Levi, Jeremy, and Mike. It was not too long after this that Levi's drinking spurred him to get sober as well. It had already ended his college career and was threatening to end more. His sponsor in AA was an electrician. After a failed GIS analyst job interview (which I totally bombed), I filled out a journeyman electrician application he gave me and nearly turned it in. It would take several years and some more life experience before I would begin to benefit from my university education.

Even in sobriety, Levi and I were true to form: we spent most nights driving backroads for miles around, eating fast food and smoking cigarettes. The biggest challenge that being home presented was finding a way to get to church. My parents by this point had taken a "don't ask, don't tell" mindset with me. They knew I didn't believe in the JW organization. I was also divorced. Two scenarios could overturn this apple cart and destroy our uneasy truce. First, if I got remarried before my ex-wife did. If she remarried first it would be viewed as her breaking the covenant, which would free me to marry. (However, if you're willing to jump through the hoops, the disfellowshipping/shunning period for adultery is usually only a year, and then you're back in good standing with the congregation, shiny new spouse and all.) The second possibility was much more ominous: getting disfellowshipped for a matter of conscience or principle, such as voting or joining another religion. This was more calculated, more willful, and unless you were willing to renounce your beliefs when caught, unforgivable. It creates a stalemate the JWs are ready to go to the mat for.

My parents were only worried about the latter possibility. They didn't badger me about JW meeting attendance, and our religious discussions avoided the kind of pointed questions that might force me to show my hand. For this, I was grateful.

For all that, family life reached its most idyllic pitch during this time. All four of us, Dad, Mom, sister, and I, lived there at the house. This was another blessed time God granted me in sobriety. My sister and I had a heartfelt rapprochement. It came to me, now that I was thinking clearly, that I had a sister. *I had a sister*: the only person in the world with the same two parents as me. And she'd always looked up to me, despite my unwillingness to be the big brother she needed me to be. I was too busy with my own friends and pursuits, unwilling to accept any inconvenience for her sake. And here she was nearly grown, and I realized I was more proud of her than I could express. She was well-adjusted, good-humored, loyal, and kind. By God's grace, I could see that now. And I could tell her that, and at least for a little while, be her big brother.

I had been a maladjusted child in many ways. I was an incorrigible idealist from a young age, jealous, selfish with my time always, and both prideful and underconfident. It seems most people remember childhood fondly, but I remember it most as a state of gnawing tension. I had kicked against the goad my whole life. Coming in conscious contact with the living God was the beginning of the healing of these wounds for which alcohol was a superficial bandage. Accordingly, the beauty of life finally began to show through to me. As I mentioned, my mother cleaned houses for a living. To pick up some extra cash, she cleaned the front office building at the place where my dad worked. Because this was done on Friday night, it made sense that the rest of us would accompany her and help. This simple manual labor in solidarity with my mother, father, and sister is my fondest memory with them. It was a simple way to help shoulder the burden, but also a way to show the kind of love best manifested in the quiet shared experience of everyday life.

Contentment is one of the greatest gifts you can give to those around you, and I believe it has power to save. It might also be termed "acquiring the Holy Spirit," such is its monumental importance. But I enjoyed it—vacuuming, windexing the glass, gathering up the trash—because we were doing it together, for one another. In sobriety I could rest in that, appreciate that, and cherish it as the moment-by-moment unfolding of an all-encompassing benevolence.

Chapter 7

Christ's Church, the Devil's Dogs, and the Unmaking of a Family

Living at home, however, did not allow me complete freedom of movement, even now. My parents weren't going to throw me out for my doubts and failure to attend meetings, but they certainly couldn't stand idly by while I went off to false religious ceremonies. And if I were to leave on a Sunday morning around 10 a.m., the destination would be pretty clear regardless of what I said. I bided my time accordingly and continued my research. When I did move out, I wanted to have some idea of which Baptist Church to start attending.

Although Catholicism was viscerally attractive, the real issue, that of faith versus works righteousness, remained solved, and for the most part my choice seemed clear. But the hound of heaven is nothing if not persistent, and I could never quite disabuse myself of this persistent fascination with the Catholic Church.

I started reading and watching debates on the topic between Protestants and Catholics. One debate I happened upon was between some Baptist (I can't even remember his name) and Brother Peter Dimond of the Holy Family Monastery in New York. Dimond took a tack I'd never considered before. He went in and showed that many of the Pauline denunciations of "works" and "law" were actually specific criticisms of the Judaizing heresy of the first century, which taught that new Christians were bound to observe the works of the *Mosaic* Law (circumcision, certain dietary restrictions, etc.). St. Paul's main point in many of these cases is to show that faith is the new justifier, the new entrance into the covenant, rather than the former prescriptions. It was also nonsensical to ask whether works do anything separate from the act of faith: works that don't flow from faith are worthless, as any Catholic would admit, but faith not manifested in works is obviously no faith at all, as many Protestants would admit.

What is not upheld by Scripture (as is more obvious in the Gospels and in places like St. James's epistle) is the idea that justifying faith could coexist with and even erase the punishment due to someone "sinning boldly," as Luther hyperbolically proclaimed. Putting all this together, it became clear that those verses which seem more Protestant are instead fully in accord with the more Catholic-sounding portions of Scripture. It, like so many Catholic answers (and like life in general) is *both/and* rather than either/or. We are saved by faith manifested in works. To separate them is a reductionistic move born of the scrupulous anxiety of one man who despaired of being "perfect, as also [the] heavenly Father is perfect" (Matthew 5:48).

All this hit me like a ton of bricks late one night as I was listening to that debate. I sat stunned as the pieces all fell into place in my mind. So I was to be Catholic after all, I thought, and suddenly my heart felt settled. But what about all the extraneous social or cultural considerations? They didn't matter, was the calming answer. Here was something to stand on, something trustworthy. The other chips could fall as they may.

I phoned the local Catholic parish the next day and got in touch with the priest. He told me to come in that day for confession and a chat, which I did. He absolved me of over a year's worth of sin as well as the semi-schismatic act of re-baptism. We discussed what was possible for my practice of the faith while living in a JW home. There was no reason, he said, at this time to declare myself a Catholic and take my punishment. It was much easier to get out of the house on Wednesday night than on Sunday morning, so he transferred my weekly Mass attendance obligation to Wednesday night. In these heavily Protestant communities, a lot of Catholic churches will do their Wednesday daily Mass in the evening to parallel the tradition of Wednesday night Bible study that many Evangelical churches observe.

An even greater peace was descending over my life. It was the deepening and broadening of that initial inbreaking that had come that night at the customer service desk. It was almost like normal life could now begin: a life with more changes on the horizon, but one in which the foundations were secure. I moved out of my parents' house and into the spare bedroom of a fellow sponsee of Eric's in Nashville, someone who had become a good friend of mine and who had several years of sobriety under his belt. He had bought a house for cheap in a rough area of South Nashville (his home had been broken into a month before I moved in and would be broken into again a month after I left). I was still working at Kroger across town since they'd held my job for me while I was in DC, and I was volunteering for an urban planning nonprofit downtown in my spare time, which matured into a paid position.

My roommate was a regular attendee at the Nashville midnight meeting, over off Nolensville Pike, so I got involved in that with him. My shifts were later in the day usually, so staying up late fit my schedule, and we'd stay up even later than midnight, hanging out at a nearby diner till the wee hours of the morning. I briefly sponsored a few guys, chaired some meetings, and generally got involved as I'd done in DC. At work I took on one overnight shift a week on Saturday nights, peeling and sticking labels all over the store. There's something enchanted about overnight and early morning work—the silence of the world, the chill of the air, the peaceful solitude and recollection that floods in naturally. I listened to Kings of Leon and Catholic apologetics on my off-brand MP3 player as I worked. This Kroger store had become a dear home and family to me over the past few years, especially in sobriety. They were an unforgettable cast of characters. There was Mr. Bob, the born-again front end supervisor of friendly ease and impeccable honesty; Mike, the plucky deadpan grocery man with white boy baller potential at the community center; Ashley, my sarcastic but devoted front end manager who always had my back; Catherine, the displaced New Orleanian with sass and a heart of gold; Cynthia, fellow Catholic and the most fun to tease, who could give as good as she got; Ms. Ruby, the tough Southern lady who had a mother's heart; and Mr. Uhles, the young store manager who was taking the management game by storm and who reminded me of my uncles on my mother's side; these and many others were people of surpassing warmth and character who I worked alongside for four and a half years, and who formed a true community. I hold in my mind the experience of this certain place at this certain time, working shoulder to shoulder with these people. It's a golden edifice, richly adorned by the Lord. It hangs there in the mind of God and, in the truthfulness of hindsight, I can see it shine forth in all its perfection.

After my all-nighter at Kroger on Saturday night, I'd change clothes in my car, grab a fast-food breakfast and coffee, and then head over to the Church of the Assumption in Germantown for Mass. I'd adopted

Assumption as my parish after attending a Traditional Latin Mass (the "Extraordinary Form") there out of curiosity. Perhaps surprisingly, I wasn't initially blown away by the beauty of the Old Mass. I'm not sure exactly what I was expecting, but when I found out it was only offered once a month, I wasn't too heartbroken. The Novus Ordo Mass on offer there was dignified and similar in style to the Extraordinary Form.

I don't say that to paint myself into the anti-Latin Mass crowd (an advantageous move these days). I say it to be honest, but also to illustrate the fact that beauty, while indeed objective and basically unchanging, is still somewhat dependent on a trained palette. It's like wine tasting—I have zero skill or experience judging wines. Pour me a glass of Romanee-Conti (I had to Google that) or a glass of Franzia, and I'll be hard-pressed to tell the difference, or even identify the various tasting notes. But that in no way means those differences are subjective, or that I couldn't, with some training, learn to perceive them. Likewise with beauty in music, visual art, liturgy, architecture, etc. Now that I've thought and studied on the subject, I do find the Latin Mass to be a stunning display, perhaps the most perfect religious choreography in existence. When done properly, it does reach out and arrest me in ways that it never could've in my former ignorance. So like all sweeping claims, my claim that "beauty is objective" needs to be couched in an understanding that subjective experience can differently perceive the objective through a mix of ignorance, lack of formation, or even willful blindness.

But I perceived that something was different about the liturgical feel of Assumption parish, and that something was vital. My baptism had taken place in a church more of the mainstream suburban vein of Catholicism that reigns virtually unchallenged in the vast majority of Novus Ordo parishes. I didn't see anything wrong with it at the time, but that was, again, owing to ignorance. I've since come to the conclusion that this disparity is one of the greatest stumbling blocks to the Catholic faith in our time. At this time I was still content to believe that, while I may have personally grown in appreciation of the traditional aesthetic, who was I to call a different style illegitimate?

At coffee hour after Mass on one of my first Sundays at Assumption, I met Mark W., who introduced me to the rest of the parish schola and got me signed up. Mark was also a convert, raised Church of Christ, so he understood somewhat the dynamic with my family. Mark and I became fast friends: he was a good bit older than me, a single man in his late forties, but he had a studied Anglo-Catholic sensibility that I was drawn to (he had spent some time as an Episcopalian).

The schola was made up of similar fellows, some with families. I was discovering that Assumption was an "intentional" community, or one based on shared interests and predilections. People of a certain mindset sought it out and congregated there. Being from a small town, I found being submerged in this element akin to being a kid in a candy store. It was the Catholic equivalent of Capitol Hill Baptist. I'm a little leerier of the artificiality of such groupings these days, but there's no denying the succor they provide to those outside the mainstream. And in time, I do believe they can solidify into something resembling normal (i.e., geographically-based) parishes.

I was introduced through singing with the Assumption schola to the riches of the Church's patrimony. We sang Gregorian chant in Latin and English—all the prescribed propers that constitute the Mass throughout the year. I remember my first traditional Easter Triduum—when the priest dropped to the floor and lay flat, I was mystified. I could feel the gravity of the event we were reliving.

Whereas before, AA was my main experience of tangible, saving faith, at Assumption I entered into the living stream of Catholicism, and everything I'd been introduced to in AA took on added depth and beauty. I had found myself thrown into the world as a confused, proto-alcoholic Jehovah's Witness boy. I found myself, circa 2012, snatched from the fires of my passions and breathing the air of God's world for the first time. Tears of thanksgiving frequently accompanied my steps.

Back at work, I was given a few manager relief shifts because they saw potential in me for the job. I had begun to despair of using my degree for anything: with the job market as it was and my lack of experience, it seemed useless. Besides, I liked my store, and by extension the company. I could see myself making a career out of grocery store management.

But a fire was burning inside me, one I hadn't dared indulge in all these years until now, when life had opened up like a vista before me. I wanted to join the military. Understand that being in the armed forces of any country is strictly forbidden by the Witnesses. They take Christ's words to be "not of the world" to mean having no active role in any government or political organization (John 15:19). It's generally one of the "notes of truth" for many of them: only Jehovah's Witnesses show Christlike love by refusing to fight in wars, which might otherwise result in Witnesses killing each other. They're not technically pacifists, though it manifests that way practically. Few of them own weapons, even guns for hunting, out of a general reticence about any sort of violence.

Needless to say, joining the military is a disfellowshipping, or shunning, offense. I hadn't allowed myself to consider it because until now I'd halfway harbored the illusion that I could remain a secret apostate for the rest of my life. You could join another religion in secret, but going to boot camp and traveling across the world on deployment were unavoidably public acts. It would spell the end of my relationship with my parents.

I've always been a fiercely idealistic person. It was that and some romanticized, adventurous fiction (*The Lord of the Rings*, for example) that pushed me over the edge, along with a desire to go in place of those who couldn't. I had of late come to realize how unbelievably blessed I was to have four fully functioning limbs, good health, and twenty-two years of life under my belt. Wasn't anything else I could hope for beyond that just icing on the cake at this point? And even if I could die doing it, what would the rest of my life be like knowing I'd selfishly hoarded my blessings, that I'd kept life in reserve?

What does self-sacrifice have to do with the US military, the greatest force of destruction on the planet (some would argue) for the past thirty years? My desire to serve wasn't a studied ideological statement or an intellectually considered position. Though probably common to all young men, there's something in the Germano-Celtic DNA, a certain fatalism, that impels us toward a fight regardless of the stakes or moral rectitude. It's not fighting just to fight or fighting out of pent-up rage or anger. It's a dispassionate passion, and there's something ennobling about it, regardless of the nefarious designs it can be put to by those in power. I believe ultimately what we did in Iraq was wrong, but the warriors who prosecuted that war on the ground are heroes to me. There's obviously a limit to this; at some point one does become culpable for participating in a thoroughly unjust war. But as of 2012, in my limited judgment, we didn't seem to be at that point. Maybe nowadays we are.

With all these ideals, I naturally gravitated towards the United States Marine Corps. Their promotionals didn't advertise the GI Bill, the exotic duty stations, or the tech I'd be working with. Instead there were three simple words: honor, courage, and commitment. They talked about doing hard things and sacrificing for the nation. The videos of the drill instructors were pretty startling, but the glory to be had, the pride of belonging, made it seem worth it. I can't remember who told who about the Marines, but soon both Levi and I had made appointments to talk to the recruiter.

Having a college degree, I briefly considered applying for Officer Candidate School. However, the physical entrance requirements were higher (I couldn't do twenty pull-ups in a row yet), and I didn't really understand what the difference was. Plus, I wanted to go to Parris Island, like in the movies—that ominous swamp where Marines are made.

We got involved at the recruiting station in the Spring of 2012 but were told we wouldn't ship out to boot camp until the fall or even the winter. This would allow us time to get physically and mentally prepared. We would be enrolled in the poolee program, which included fitness and knowledge tests. Occasionally we had to go to Clarksville for larger events, but in general we were local with the boys, learning the ropes from our devil-may-care recruiter. He'd chug a Monster energy drink and then bust out twenty-three pull-ups while smoking a cigarette (I later learned this wasn't remarkable in the Marine Corps). The recruiter arranged it so that Levi and I would almost certainly have the same ship date for boot camp. Deep down I was anxious about it, but knowing that there'd be at least one familiar face there with me was comforting.

As the months dragged toward our ship date (December, we were told), the looming issue of my family's reaction dominated my consciousness. I thought of various alibis: what if I said I had gotten a job contracting with the military to plan their bases? I floated this to my mom, saying I was considering such a position, to gauge her response. It seemed like such a story could *work*, in that it might be sufficiently neutral sounding to keep me from getting shunned. But was it sufficiently *true* enough not to be a lie? Well, not really. And even if it was, how would I control the leak of pictures and information such that there was no evidence of my enlisting?

It soon became apparent to me that I would have to tell them. There'd be no other honest way to explain my sudden disappearance and non-responsiveness: cell phones and email were not allowed at Marine boot camp. I had to approach this cautiously: the moment I told them would be the moment the machinery of shunning would be activated, culminating in a public announcement to the congregation that would cause the cessation of all normal contact. My sister was getting married in September, and I was supposed to be in the ceremony. The longer I waited to tell them, the more normal life I could live with them in the meantime.

Why was I doing this? Would it be worth it? If my family really mattered to me, couldn't I just keep my mouth shut, practice my religion outside their view, and refrain from public displays like joining the Marine Corps that would force their hand?

No, I couldn't. The early Christians could've outwardly performed the required emperor worship rituals while inwardly repudiating them and professing Christ, but they didn't, instead choosing to publicly proclaim their faith and accept certain death. Without that gory display, Christianity would've been worthless, and probably just another footnote of history. This is paradoxically how Christianity affirms life: by embracing death. A principle, a belief, a being-towards-the-world, to put it in Martin Heidegger's terms, that does not rise above the survival instinct is by default subsumed under the mundane, the changeable, the negotiable. It is part of the world. Only by being worth dying for does a notion become transcendent, i.e., worth serving rather than using. Christianity is exactly this type of thing. My fandom for University of Memphis football, for instance, is not. Neither are a lot of my political beliefs. In many cases these things serve me, not the other way around. But the Gospel, if it truly infiltrates the mind, holds it captive. It becomes the lodestar, the fixed point, the foundation.

One who dies for Christianity affirms life because life requires Christianity. Life is a meaningless void or an impenetrable enigma without Christ. Evil entered this world because love requires freedom, and freedom admits the possibility of evil. God is love, an eternal communion of persons, and his creation is meant to mirror and participate in this never-ending exchange. As we see in Genesis and as we feel in our bones, something went wrong with life: we see what should be, and it is not. We see the potential perfection but experience the very real lack: fear, selfishness, exploitation, alienation, despair, hate, death. And we know, when we're honest, that just like our first parents, the capacity for not only great love but also for unspeakable evil exists deep in all of us. Life is this knowledge and experience.

But life contains a story within it that changes everything: that of Jesus of Nazareth, who claimed divine paternity and prerogatives and of whom great miracles were reported, including his triumph over the grave by a literal flesh and blood resurrection. The power behind this event impelled hundreds and thousands to go joyfully to their deaths with his name on their lips. This event revealed the story at the heart of the world: that our blameless Maker came into our misery and absorbed our evil onto himself, in a completely gratuitous, inexplicably merciful act of self-oblation. That the King of the Universe submitted to being mockingly crowned by his creatures while they spit upon and slapped him and led him to the place where they would brutally murder him.

The story speaks to us at levels we can't penetrate rationally. Why did God have to come and "take it" for us? Why couldn't he just use his magical powers and snap his fingers and say we were all saved (or at least the good ones among us)?

Is that how anything in this world works, though? When your spouse hurts you, deals unlovingly with you, you have a choice: repay the evil with equal force, or absorb it and forgive. And that second option, while ultimately the smoother path, initially *hurts*—it involves suffering. It hurts to be the bigger man; it's hard not to retaliate. To do so is to do no less than to take the evil in, contain it, and snuff it out—to stop the cycle, in short. But not without pain.

This is the "economy" of good and evil, the spiritual currency we all trade in. God couldn't ignore it any more than he could create a rock too heavy for himself to lift. To expect such would be to expect logical absurdity from the Source of all light, life, and reason. So down the All-Holy One came, into the heart of darkness. We therefore have a Savior acquainted with our plight—acquainted because he freely took it upon himself and worked it out within his own person, even within his own sinless body. Turn the other cheek, surrender the cloak, go the second mile (Matthew 5:38-41)—these are not just sermons he gave, but battles he fought and won. The ancient evil, the serpent's curse, was loosed upon him at our hands. He did not turn and smite us, justified as that would've been, but rather opened himself up and drew down the ugly dysfunction, the unpardonable wickedness, on himself, and through great, compassionate suffering, nullified its spell forever. By his divine power he triumphed over it, raised his scarred but glorious body up as a victory standard over all the earth, and offered a share in his suffering and conquering flesh to all men, so that they might imitate him in absorbing and cutting off evil in every age.

In the light of this story, the story of each person's life makes sense. You can now become part of the salvation of everything by taking up your part of his sufferings, by entering into your personal passion play. If you're mystically united to him, you will triumph. And following him, you will die—whether at the hands of your enemies or because of the lingering effects of the curse—but as he did, you can now embrace a courageous, even reckless stance towards death, which is the secret to being alive.

Fear then is banished; death's sting is muted. The central fact of life is not staying alive, but living and dying for something greater than life. Dying in Christ is more real than consciousness. Placing conscious physical life at the pinnacle of the hierarchy of values cheapens not only that consciousness but all values.

So if a Christian is not heedless of death and discomfort for the sake of Christianity, without which his life and comfort collapse in on themselves as pitiful diversions, then he has not entered into Christianity. Thus martyrdom. Thus the realization that I couldn't be a secret Catholic to keep the peace with my family. What would yanking down all our religious art every time they came over or studiously avoiding posting a family Christmas photo say about my relationship to this value hierarchy? It would say that life and comfort and worldly benefits (even wonderful ones like the love and companionship of family) are greater than the only thing that keeps them from becoming mere temporary pleasures. That would be an absurdity, and a gross injustice to God. Martyrdom is Christianity because Christianity is the story of God's martyrdom. And martyrdom, or at least sacrifice, has been at the foundation of all human culture since the dawn of civilization. For whatever reason, I was being called to a very specific martyrdom: the oblation of the family ties I cherished so deeply. To try to keep both my faith and my family would've made a lie out of them both. I didn't have to call them up today and spill the beans, but the conclusion was inescapable. They would have to know. If now was the appointed time to embark on a great military adventure, it was also the time to make a stand for my faith, once and for all. Either of these actions would bring the judgment.

My sister was married that fall to her husband at a vineyard in West Tennessee. It was the last time I would see my family gathered in one place together. My part was to walk my mother in. One of my uncles gave the sermon. The highlight from my point of view was the father-daughter dance. They danced wonderfully. It had been rough on Dad seeing his eighteen-year-old daughter courting and getting married so quickly. The dance seemed to represent a graceful surrender of his beloved daughter. For those who knew them both well, I doubt there was a dry eye.

The wedding experience confirmed the wisdom of waiting to come clean. I would've been barred from it had they known my plans prior to the ceremony. As it turned out, I waited to tell them until the last possible moment.

My grandmother on my dad's side had dementia pretty bad. She'd been in decline since her stroke a few years before, but after my grandfather died, she really took a turn for the worse. My dad, aunt, and uncle sold her house in rapidly gentrifying Sylvan Park and used the proceeds to put her in assisted living (coincidentally, Mary Queen of Angels). I don't necessarily blame them for that, but I sincerely hope we can avoid putting my parents in a nursing home. I know it's hard, especially when there are memory and behavioral issues, but it seems like a betrayal of nature.

Grandma ended up biting someone, I believe, at MQA, which resulted in her expulsion. One day in early December, we had to get her moved into a new facility out in another county. It was a sad day, and an ignominious finale to what had become a very pitiful phase of her life. But what was weighing on my mind even more heavily that day was the news I would be sharing with my family that night. It would be the night I declared myself a Roman Catholic before my parents and told them of my intention to become a Marine. Why this night? Because I was leaving for medical processing and Parris Island in the morning!

It was on a blackened stretch of I-40 on the way home when I finally spoke up. "Dad, I have something to tell you," I said, my voice pregnant with foreboding.

"What, Son," he said flatly. I could tell he sensed the danger.

"I want to tell you that I'm Catholic, and also that I joined the Marine Corps and am leaving for boot camp in the morning." Like the shot heard 'round the world, the statement pierced the air and hung there.

There was a pause. "I figured you had gone and done something like join the Marines," he said, sighing. "I wasn't expecting you to tell me you were Catholic." The dark woods rushed past our windows.

"How did you know about the Marines?" I asked.

"I'm not stupid. I could tell something was going on, what with Levi joining. I can't understand how you'd become Catholic, though. After our talks with Burt, I thought it was clear."

Burt was a scholar-type former JW who my dad had taken me to once to try to talk some sense into me. I didn't learn until later that he was no longer a Witness. His qualification had been that he was still a non-trinitarian.

We had engaged in prooftexting that went nowhere and left me looking stubborn and recalcitrant.[1]

"That wasn't a fair debate," I said. "I couldn't really argue like a Catholic or else I'd have been found out. That's the kind of interaction you get when you threaten people with shunning if they disagree with you—they can't be completely honest."

No reply. No point now, I guess.

"You know what this means," he said.

"Yeah, I know. I don't agree with it but I know." The woods whirring past outside seemed as dark and threatening as ever.

When we finally pulled into the driveway my heart was heavy with the task awaiting me. Momma came out of her room, oblivious, asking about something for the next day. I told her straightforwardly. A look of total despondency invaded her features. She barely spoke, then whimpered. When we hugged I could feel the lifelessness in her body.

I slept in my sister's recently vacated room that night. My room across the hall was part lounge, part storage now. I had started reading *The Fellowship of the Ring* a few months before: motivation for the great adventure I was embarking on. I was at the point where Frodo is hiding from the ring wraiths in the Shire on his way to Bree. Adventures, when they become real, suddenly become dangerous and scary. They give you that sinking feeling in your stomach. To leave the Shire, to bid goodbye to friends, work, home, way of life—and to bid my family farewell in this terrible, permanent way—at that moment, I couldn't understand it. I lay under the covers and trembled.

The morning brought a stiff, painful goodbye. Momma was shell-shocked, non-responsive. Daddy was stern but unresistant. There was no acrimony, no pleas for reconsidering. Dad had me sign a statement saying something to the effect that I renounced the Witness organization. He said it would make the process of my leaving "easier." I guess that means it made it easier to proclaim me shunned, but I didn't care at this point.

When Levi's car pulled up outside, they told me they loved me, and we said goodbye. It was goodbye in a more fateful, final sense than any other type of goodbye, save for that which comes before death. For that reason it carried behind it dammed up emotions waiting to burst forth, but they had to be held in check. We couldn't let ourselves experience everything

---

1. For a defense of the Trinity that I think adequately comprehends and addresses Witness concerns, refer to the Appendix.

this goodbye meant. Goodbye to twenty-two years of shared life, familiarity, and mutual helpfulness. Goodbye to carefree timelessness together, and to beach and Smoky Mountain trips. Goodbye to just dropping in, to impromptu pantry raids. Goodbye to phone calls and funny texts. Goodbye to working alongside one another, goodbye to helping with a project or the daily chores. Goodbye to inside jokes with a sibling and pushing each other's buttons. Goodbye to the guidance of a father and the ambitious plans of a young man. Goodbye to the concern and care of a mother and the carelessness of a son. Goodbye to an entire world that we were all essential inhabitants of, and goodbye to the natural expectation that it was good and wasn't going anywhere. There was so much life ripped away from all three of us with that goodbye that a sudden bereavement is probably the only thing it could be compared to. And yet, it was in many ways worse because we all knew it would be accomplished, not by some inscrutable act of God or nature, but by our own hands.

Levi asked how it was. I said it was pretty rough. I felt like I'd gotten the wind knocked out of me. I was lucky there was no time to process it. We were soon swept up in the hustle and bustle of MEPS, the medical processing stage of intake, over off Donelson Pike. You strip down, you walk like a duck, you wait for hours. I can't recall whether we had to stay a night at the Millennium Maxwell House Hotel before or after MEPS processing, but for some reason that was part of the process. I thought that night about dying on some foreign battlefield, estranged from my own mother.

When the time finally came to depart for Parris Island, we were standing outside MEPs with Levi's family. Particularly touching was Levi's father: he was a tough man, a factory worker and union organizer, who had rebuilt a '67 Mustang engine. I'd never seen him show much emotion, but here he was, so simultaneously proud and concerned for us that tears were streaming down his face. I'd like to think a part of that was a feeling of solicitude for me after what had happened with my parents. Levi's folks had been out of the Witness religion for several years now. There was a certain solidarity that existed among us—refugees and vagabonds to our former community and way of life. You feel a special bond with people you grow with. We were friends because of the Kingdom Hall, but now, in the outer darkness together, we were something more like family. I hugged them like they were my own parents as they saw us off.

The journey was a long van ride heading southeast through Tennessee and South Carolina. I remember very little about it. The only thing that stands out is our "last supper" at a Golden Corral somewhere in Carolina. We were told to dine like kings, for it would be our last free and easy meal. I stuffed myself to gorging and smoked two cigarettes outside the restaurant. Then we loaded into the multi-passenger van and sped off into the night. It seemed like we took only backroads. The driver assumed a gruff manner, so we all straightened up and sat in silence. The big white van hurtled at breakneck speeds, which heightened the tension. As we drove on, the landscape slowly flattened out and took on a swampy, coastal aspect.

We arrived, of course by design, at Marine Corps Recruit Training Depot Parris Island in the middle of the night; probably two or three in the morning. A drill instructor sporting a Smokey the Bear hat slid open the sliding door and shouted at us to quickly exit the van and take our places on the yellow footprints outside on the asphalt. I reflected on the surreal experience of seeing myself in that iconic moment. We were then herded into the building through some "hatches" (doors) that we would never walk through again. The doors symbolize the leaving behind of the old life, so that once you become a Marine, you avoid those doors ever after in honor of the transformation that's taken place. These were my first small initiations into a truly traditionalist organization, which would have profound effects on my worldview.

We shuffled from station to station through a dizzying array of nondescript rooms and bays, filling out paperwork, collecting gear, and being yelled at. Everything was rushed, urgent, with no room for error. We had no idea where we were, what time it was, or when we would be able to rest. We must've been kept awake for over forty-eight hours in all. They buzzed our heads, and one boy passed out. I noticed that even the civilian barbers had little patience or use for us: everyone was snapping orders. When you live so much of your life in polite suburban society, it's easy to forget how disconcerting treatment like this is.

The first week, aside from the initial shock, wasn't *that* bad. I remember thinking as we marched to the "chow hall" (the cafeteria) one night that I could do this. The temporary drill instructors who had care of us did drop ominous hints, though, about what would happen when we got our drill instructors. I didn't know what that meant, but I didn't have to wait long to find out. On the first Saturday they crowded us into our squad bay (the long hall-like room with all the bunk beds). In marched four drill instructors we'd never seen before. They popped to parade rest (feet spread, hands clasped behind the back) and their names were read out. These were the drill instructors (DIs) for Platoon 2018 for the December-March training cycle. Every thought of "this isn't so bad" or "I got this" evaporated within the next thirty minutes. A whirlwind of chaos erupted: the four DIs exploded onto us, screaming, chasing us, ordering us to pick up and dump our foot lockers, to sprint up and down the squad bay, and to scream at the top of our lungs every response. The best hope was to try to blend in and avoid individual attention, but as the pandemonium wore on, I realized the chances of that were slim to none. My singular memory of that day was watching Levi being accosted by a DI with repeated orders to scream "Explode!" ever more loudly ("explode" was what we were to yell after the DI said, "Instruct": it meant we were to "explode" over to the place where he was and into a learning frame of mind. Usually our "explode" would be met with a "get back" from the DI, which meant we were lacking in volume or intensity and needed to try again). There was my best friend since age eight, in this same unbelievable situation as me, off behind the group (the rest of us had since "exploded" satisfactorily and were kneeling at the DI's feet taking in instruction), hoarsely screaming "explode" over and over (he had been told not to quit). The tragicomic absurdity suddenly got to me, and I snickered. Of course, I was soon sprinting back and forth and being forced to hold my rifle out in front of me (try just holding your plain arm out in front of you for any length of time to understand the simple genius of this form of torture).

The next morning we were begrudgingly given about an hour and a half for worship by the DIs. We were marched to an auditorium for Mass (Levi went despite not being Catholic). We only had a few moments to talk freely before Mass started. As we reflected on the past twenty-four hours, we laughed so hard we cried—or maybe we laughed to keep from crying. It was the strangest mix of bemusement and bewilderment I've ever experienced. Boot camp *was* going to be as bad as they said, but it was also going to be comedic gold. You really didn't know whether to laugh or cry, but judging by the fact that there were twelve weeks left, the latter seemed more appropriate at the time.

Our platoon was made up almost entirely of good old boys from Tennessee, Kentucky, and Alabama. It helped that we were braving this new environment with the same type of people we'd grown up with—anything familiar was something to hold on to. The thing about Marine Corps Recruit Training is that it just doesn't stop: you get the aforementioned religious time on Sunday morning and one hour of "free time" per night (which is often abbreviated or interrupted based on unsatisfactory performance).

Otherwise you're "on" every second of the day: running, screaming, shooting, marching, trying to stay awake in a class, or being IT'd. IT or incentive/intensive training, means you get personal attention from the DI as he calls out rapid fire exercise commands at you that get more difficult as you fail to respond quickly enough. "High knees! Push! Plank! Mountain climbers!" and so on, for five to ten minutes. You get punished with IT, but many times you're just in the wrong place at the wrong time, and here you go off to the sandpit or the quarterdeck (the places where IT customarily takes place). All of this is meant to simulate the chaos, stress, and haphazardness of war. You learn to unflinchingly follow orders and focus your mind on the task at hand amidst din and destruction.

Physically the most difficult aspect for me wasn't IT or PT (the regular physical training), but humps. Humps are hikes with a weighted backpack and rifle, sometimes also with flack and Kevlar (our body armor). These forced marches would go for miles, and my back would invariably be on fire almost immediately after we started. I'm proud to say I never dropped out of a hike, though my abhorrence of them would continue throughout my Marine Corps career. I don't know if there was something wrong with me or if it felt that way for everyone, but it was excruciating.

Drill and ceremony (D&C) is a huge part of boot camp—every spare moment is filled with drill practice. There's a big final drill competition at the end that the drill instructors train recruits for, and so they're fierce about perfecting their technique. It's probably one of the greatest centers of D&C excellence and tradition on the planet, and I've longed to return to the island to view the displays as a spectator one day.

Marine Corps Recruit Training is thirteen weeks long, making it the longest non-special forces basic training in the world. I won't lie: it was probably the hardest thing I've ever done. In addition to being stuck in this pressure cooker of stress for so long, the only contact you have with the outside world is via letter writing. Of course, I had no such correspondence with my own family. Luckily, I had met a Catholic lady through church circles with two boys about my age who had agreed to write to me during boot camp so that I would have letters from home to look forward to. And write she did, so that we developed a friendship that resulted in her becoming an adopted mom of sorts. Their house became a place for me to land when I was in town. I even spent several holidays and a family beach vacation with them. The manner in which they took me in and treated me as one of their own was truly touching.

There are many great detailed recountings of Marine Corps boot camp out there, and my experience differed little, so I won't rehash every episode, but there were many unforgettable moments, from the maddening games the DIs would play with us (like ordering us to dump all of our belongings in a pile and then giving us about a minute to sort them out), to the tear gas chamber, to repelling (I got stuck hanging forty feet in the air—I'm still not sure how I got myself down), to the obstacle courses, to the food- and sleep-deprived Crucible event at the end. It was the ultimate proving ground, the quintessential rite of passage. I had had no such experience growing up. I imagine sports or boy scouts provides that in some measure for many boys, but Witnesses are barred from all that. Boys have a deep hunger for it, though. Look to any "primitive" culture on earth (and I say "primitive" in quotes because in reality *we* are much more primitive when it comes to understanding human nature and the deeper needs of man): at some point in the teenage years, every boy in these cultures is put through a trying ordeal. They enter it as a boy but exit it as a man, with all the rights and privileges thereunto pertaining. This gets to the essence of what masculinity is—not just a set of traits (greater physical strength, more aggressiveness, more emotional compartmentalization, etc.), but a precarious social position based on the discharge of duties in service to the community. The duties are self-sacrifice and the burden of leadership. Just like the coveted Eagle, Globe, & Anchor bestowed on each Marine, at which moment he becomes a Marine, so is masculinity earned, never given. This fact is illustrated by how many grown men we have walking around our society today who are anything but that. Granted, there has been a concerted effort to stamp this awareness out of men and demonize masculinity while forcing it on women to the detriment of femininity, so further scapegoating is hardly called for, but the sad fact remains.

The Marine Corps models how to make boys into men: test them to their absolute limits, and then bestow upon them the honor they've earned and must be ever vigilant and diligent to keep. If we cannot stomach the demands of masculinity—either the trials and dangers necessary to achieve it, or the honors and privileges necessary to motivate it, then we will continue to fail our boys and young men. We will continue to have men who do little more than what they're told and meekly acquiesce to their abolition.

Chapter 8

Adventure and the Burning Path

Alice, my adoptive mother figure, came with Mark to my boot camp graduation—surely one of the most welcome days of every Marine's life. The precision, force, and exactitude with which we marched across that parade deck must've been a sight to behold. After a well-deserved ten days of leave, we were off to combat school (MCT) in North Carolina. Levi and I were placed in separate platoons there. MCT was less stressful but more demanding in other ways: longer, harder marches, more technical training to master, less sleep. But unlike boot camp, it was not segregated by sex, meaning females were in our platoon. The physical training regimen therefore had to be reduced in intensity—many times, on runs for instance, we had to circle up and jog in place while we waited for the women to catch up. This, combined with the caloric-rich and sugar-filled MREs (Meals-Ready-to-Eat) we were fed caused me to actually gain weight at MCT. Besides changing the training dynamic, the co-ed nature of MCT also resulted in rumors of lurid port-a-john trysts.

We trained on all sorts of weapons—my job was going to be military intelligence, but all such non-infantry Marines have to learn the basics of combat at MCT. On rare occasions we got a hot breakfast at the chow hall—mornings I relished—and usually CNN was on. I saw from that chow hall the election of Pope Francis as Supreme Pontiff, signified by the white smoke over the Vatican. It was interesting to have a personal stake in such an international event now. It's what I imagine it feels like to be a Brit watching events involving the British royal family. Here was what amounted to a monarch of sorts, who I was beholden to in some respect.

Intelligence training for Marines takes place at Virginia Beach, so I continued my trek up the eastern seaboard once MCT was completed. There was a great backlog of students waiting to be trained, so we were told we'd probably be on base for nine months—six months of waiting in addition to the three months of actual training. Also, we weren't allowed a car, so every trip off base occurred in a taxi and only during "libo" (liberty) times. But the base was located on the coastline, so we had free and easy access to the beach.

I was called one day into the commander's office and told my grandmother had died and that my family wished for me to be allowed to travel back home for the funeral. I was told that I would be released for this and that I should put in for bereavement leave immediately. In a day or so I taxied to the Virginia Beach airport and hopped on a plane for Nashville. My thought as we touched down at BNA was just how green Middle Tennessee was compared to the low country back east. It looked like the Garden of Eden from the air.

The visit was like a garden, too, because Jehovah's Witness shunning has loopholes. For instance, if you have business dealings with the shunned, or if some emergency occurs (like a death or catastrophic illness), the rules are suspended and normal relations resume for the duration of the event. In this case, I had a pass that was good for the four days I was home. My family acted totally normal toward me. Toward the end, though, Dad and I were driving on the interstate again, and he said to me, "You know that after this week, it's lights out. We go back to radio silence, for your own good."

"I know," I said. "I know those are the rules you have to follow."

I don't know why my response was so passive. Why did I roll over so easily? Why didn't I push back instead of adopting such a fatalistic attitude toward what they were doing?

In those early days, I was somehow resigned to my fate. Maybe I found it somewhat romantic, in the heroic sense. It was almost like when two skilled warriors meet in battle. Despite the fact that they're about to fight to the death, they do not hate but actually respect and even admire one another. At the time I somewhat admired the fortitude of someone who could cut his own child off out of conviction. On the other hand, perhaps the years of incomprehensible silence hadn't ground away my optimism yet. Back then it still seemed possible they'd come to their senses.

As close as I'd been to my grandmother growing up, I don't think her death had a huge impact on me. Her slow slide into the madness of dementia had the effect of gradually removing her as I knew her from my life. Sadly, what dominated my mind while home was not mourning her passing and celebrating her life, but the future of my own status in the family. I returned to Virginia dejected.

I met a lot of enduring friends in intel school. It was called the NMITC (Navy-Marine Intelligence Training Center), and people referred to their time there as NMITC High, and not without reason. It was co-ed, with all the requisite drama, and it was an awful lot like high school—classes, projects, being seen at the mall on the weekends, and parties—only with marching and intense mandatory beach workouts thrown in. A lot of the Marines were younger than me as well. I feel like I went through a second high school here, only sober this time and more sure of myself. There's a vivacity to such periods of life—a pop music-driven zest for the moment, for the weekend, for the scene. It's a headstrong, pack mentality among boys, and the members of the pack live for their nights. The mind is positively alive with the possibilities of life—chiefly romantic ones. Peacocking is essential. You feel the power, freedom, and caprice of youth in seasons like that.

I felt all this again, getting dressed to the nines and riding with the boys out to the mall to catch a movie, and then to the chicken place for wings. Marines on the town are a dangerous thing, but there was only one fight I can remember. I saw so many movies that summer. Back on base we walked to chow (I cherished my big, leisurely breakfast now after I'd been deprived at boot camp and MCT); to our make-work jobs, which kept us busy before classes started in the fall; to the beach; to the bowling alley; to the recreation center for computers, haircuts, and Subway sandwiches; and to Mass on Sundays (I was the only one that did that). We were MAT (Marines Awaiting Training), and we were living our best lives.

Full of such vitality and virility, I naturally surveyed the dating landscape. But there were no Catholic women to be found. So, not having a car or the ability to venture further afield, I signed up for Catholic Match and met a girl from the upper Midwest. The relationship, despite being long distance, progressed rapidly. I was fully alive now, or so I felt: I had the great dangerous mission abroad, the ride or die brotherhood I'd always longed for, and the sweetheart back on the homefront.

Classes finally began. We were Red Platoon, and we were learning how to gather and analyze the most important commodity on the battlefield—information. It could take many forms, so our task was theoretically endless, only capped by the constraints of our capabilities and the limits of our personal commitment to saving lives. History, politics, technology, psychology—nothing was unimportant. Here, running along the misty coastline on some morning PT surveying the choppy Atlantic, over which the fiery sun was peeking and across which lay the vast, dangerous world of all our potential targets, I was finally caught up in the great adventure I'd sought.

Red Platoon, unlike the other platoons, had a class instructor who seemed more like a drill instructor. She would make us do high knees during class and would punish us for not covering and aligning the toilet paper rolls under our sinks properly. This may sound like par for the course in the Marine Corps, but in this type of highly technical training environment, it ended up being a liability. We would be at the classroom building from seven in the morning to nine at night most days of the week trying to meet her impossible deadlines. The other platoons weren't run like that—the focus was more on learning the intelligence craft. She was removed about halfway through because someone in our platoon produced damning evidence she'd gone too far in some area. Looking back, I guess it seems silly to be surprised about the Marine Corps being unreasonable or hard (that's kind of the point), but it did seem unnecessary for Red Platoon to be so completely different from the other ones. She was not without her fans in the platoon, though—she spoke incessantly about us being "family" (we had to eat our meals together, for instance), and many of the female Marines sympathized with her. Like I said, common mess, shared suffering—these are required tactics for building unit cohesion, but that wasn't really the point of our training at NMITC. Maybe it should've been.

When our extended stay at Virginia Beach came to a close, it was off to our actual units, finally. I placed high enough in the class to be able to pick an infantry unit—these were the most coveted spots because they were the most "Marine." I was bussed back down the coast to Camp Lejeune, North Carolina, not too far north of Wilmington. Levi and his wife (they'd gotten married on his boot leave and had a newborn baby girl) allowed me to crash with them at their base housing for a few days as I got processed into my unit and assigned a place in the barracks. Third Battalion, Eighth Marines was to be my permanent home, headquartered at a newer complex on base.

I was part of the S-2 (Intelligence) shop of the battalion. As such we participated in all the major field operations but day-to-day spent most of our time in an office setting, preparing briefs for the commander and doing research. Exactitude was the name of the game, whether it was accuracy and polish while delivering a brief or literal polish while scrubbing a floor. That's what's important to understand: even if you're not laying down rounds on a 240 all day, being a Marine still affects everything you do. It's a mindset of never taking shortcuts, never making excuses, and always ruthlessly pursuing excellence. If you didn't anticipate some question and have an answer ready, or if you left something unclear in the presentation, or there were typos, the corporals and sergeants would rip you apart at the practice brief. It was an atmosphere where your feelings mattered not one bit: all that mattered was perfection. When you're lazy, Marines die, we were told. Through repeated harshness, we were molded to understand that the pang of injured pride that welled up every time we were abruptly interrupted and sharply corrected was our greatest enemy. Do it right the first time, then, if you don't like that feeling. Our wider culture these days is so finely attuned to feelings that what I'm describing can be very off-putting. But the societal slide into incompetence and the eggshells we have to walk on should illustrate the wisdom of the Marine Corps approach, at least in some contexts. We are becoming so bound and gagged by sensitivity that we're even content to deny objective reality if to do so would increase the sum total of "inclusion" in the world. Thank God the Marine Corps valued "facts over feelings," as cliché as that is to say. It taught me a work ethic I've leaned on ever since.

This was also the Marine Corps of the Marine Corps: an infantry battalion. That meant it was all-male, with a lot of yelling, cussing, and brutality. But it also meant true brotherhood and rock-solid unit cohesion. Especially for those of us living in the barracks, which most times resembled a frat house (except for on Field Day, the weekly white-gloved deep clean of every work and living space within the battalion). Social interaction among Marines is unbelievably crude, yet refreshingly honest. It's a curious phenomenon: the higher the testosterone level, the greater the frequency of ironic homosexual jokes and behavior, with the Marines leaving nothing to be desired there. It's also almost impossible not to smoke, swear, and use filthy turns of phrase.

There's a lot of hand-wringing in conservative Christian circles about such behavior among our fighting men (and the "lower classes" generally). Of course ideally I'd like to see that cleaned up, with a greater sense of propriety prevailing. But as I said, there's a very endearing lack of all pretense within such groups. There's also cynicism, but it's lived with a type of openness that I think is closer to God than the stuffy respectability of the upper middle-class work-from-home set (myself included). It soon became clear in my unit that I was a convicted Catholic. I certainly received some good-natured ribbing for my beliefs, but at bottom the nonreligious ones sensed there was something worth respecting about religiosity, even if they despaired of ever coming to personal faith themselves.

I lucked out in that Josh, a good friend from intel school who was in my shop, had had a conversion to Evangelicalism. We teamed up, and with the tacit blessing of one of our Staff NCOs who was also a Christian, openly started discouraging immoral behavior. Josh was married and lived off base, so I got my mail delivered at his house. He came from a small town nestled in the hills along the Ohio River, and he was one of those honest, tough, and loyal-to-a-fault Midwestern Americans so common in our armed forces. Dramatically different in origin was Carlos, a formerly gang-affiliated half-black, half-Mexican Angelino from Compton. I never heard the end of it from him about my Tennessee roots, but I came right back at him about his "straight outta Compton" background. Carlos was constantly laughing and joking, but he always knew when it was time to lock it up and put nose to the grindstone. The S-2 Alpha for our shop (the officer underneath the captain) was a mustang (a former enlisted man turned officer) from Alabama who had served multiple combat tours in Iraq. He knew how to lead Marines, and we all respected the hell out of him.

News soon came that our unit would be deploying to Europe on what was called the Black Sea Rotational Force (BSRF). My eyes widened and my imagination ran wild when they told me. Spots weren't guaranteed, though, and would be based on merit. I redoubled my efforts and eventually secured a spot.

This presented some problem, though, for my relationship. My girlfriend had moved in with her aunt and uncle in Greenville, South Carolina, which was about a five- or six-hour drive from Camp Lejeune. I'd spent a few days during Christmas time with her and her family, and things seemed shaky afterward. She had taken the plunge, though, and moved closer, and I bit the bullet and made the long drive almost every weekend. It proved to be just what we needed, and our relationship intensified. Things were moving quite fast, and they were about to speed up.

The dates for our deployment finally got set: March to September, six months total. Training schedules picked up as we entered the "work up" phase before a deployment. Would an eight-month-old relationship survive a six-month separation? We both knew one way to ensure that it would: get engaged. She came during one of the final weekends before we were to ship out and stayed at Levi and his wife's place over in base housing. I got a glass bottle of Coke, drank it, and stuck the ring and a note inside. I had Levi go place the bottle by a fountain in the park and then she and I took an evening stroll. She "found" the bottle and I popped the question, and we arrived back at the house with the news that we were engaged.

Having thus locked down a sweetheart on the home front, I was ready for our great patriotic adventure. We stayed first at Cherry Point, in a holding building adjacent to the tarmac, for what seemed like forever. Generous snacks were provided to us by the good people of the USO, so we didn't want for food. There's so much waiting in the military, especially when you're in transit. You're always waiting for "word" on what's happening next because generally you're kept in the dark. When it seemed like we were stalled for a while, we would sleep—then wake up groggy and gross. This feeling wasn't helped by the steady diet of cigarettes and Monster energy drinks that supplemented our snacking, plus coffee in the mornings. Finally, we were ordered out. We strode proudly to the waiting charter plane, rifles in hand. I remember the gigantic air bus gleaming gloriously in the Carolina sun, and the impressively tall roll-away stairs we climbed to board it.

Since we took a chartered plane, the flight was actually very comfortable, and there was enough room for most of us to spread out and sleep overnight. I read, while most listened to music or watched movies. We briefly stopped over in Germany but were only treated to the inside of another holding facility, where unenthusiastic Germans offered us snacks again. The final leg of our journey was much shorter—we were going to a small village near Constanța, Romania.

We touched down in cold, snowy weather and quickly set about getting our weapons checked in at our makeshift armory. It was a treeless landscape—I could make out through the falling snow rolling plains in all directions. We were on an Army base, and probably quite outnumbered by soldiers and airmen. The buildings were all Quonset huts and warehouses, but they had a slightly cartoonish look about their metal finishing that made them seem foreign to me.

We worked longer and harder on deployment, but we still had the weekends off. The Quonset huts consisted of large rooms containing eight or so bunk beds accessed off a main hall with a communal bathroom in the center. We were told not to drink the water, so plentiful bottled water was provided. I was in a room with Carlos, our corporal James from Pennsylvania, a corn-fed former body builder from Kansas named Marshall, and another Hispanic Californian also named Carlos, among others. Marshall led us every morning around four to the gym for power lifting. For thirty minutes before that, I would video chat my fiancée. This necessitated me going to bed around eight each night to avoid losing sleep. To lift properly, the thing to do was to listen to fast rock or metal, and so I downloaded Stone Temple Pilots' first album. Every time I hear those slamming chords and angry lyrics, I'm taken back to those workouts. I also listened to C.T. Fletcher, a big, powerful black man who would scream and cuss at you to push harder. Between the two of them it must've worked, because I lifted more there than I ever have before or since.

After a steaming shower came the well-earned full breakfast. The chow hall was a dream, with a 24/7 sandwich bar and custom omelet service in the mornings. We'd each eat something like a five- or six-egg omelet, bacon or sausage and pancakes, along with hot black coffee. Getting there early was worth it to truly enjoy the sumptuous spread. The long day in the office began next, with constant research and briefs on all the neighboring countries we were training with or monitoring. I learned a good deal about that part of the world. In the evenings I would do some form of cardio (our PT tests required that type of fitness). Bedtime, as I said, came early with headphones in and white noise cranked up—I was in a room full of Marines who didn't share my commitment to a good night's sleep.

On the weekends we'd split a cab and make for Constanța on the Black Sea coast, where Jason and the Argonauts landed with the Golden Fleece over three thousand years prior. The city was truly ancient, and it had Greek heritage, which was discernible in the sunbaked old town. The towering "casino" building, which sat astride the harbor, was the most significant architectural landmark, but well-designed and sometimes very beautiful Romanian Orthodox churches dotted the cityscape as well. This was my first real exposure to Eastern Orthodox Christianity, and I came away with the impression that Romania was still a Christian country. I witnessed someone cross himself three times on the bus when we passed a church. There were also numerous roadside shrines featuring icons and exquisite carving work. When once I wandered into the cathedral in Constanța, I was presented with monks serving an elaborate sung liturgy complete with incense, in the middle of the day, with no apparent regard for anyone who might be watching them. On a separate occasion, I went to the nearest parish in the adjacent village on a Sunday while the Divine Liturgy was being served. The congregants enthusiastically greeted my companion and me and ushered us to the front of the church, where we were given blessed bread to eat. When the priest settled into a long homily in Romanian, we politely excused ourselves amid much protest. At least in Romania, Eastern Orthodoxy sure looked, acted, and quacked like you'd think ancient Christianity would. Strangely enough, however, the thought of converting to it never occurred to me (that would come later). This was just "their" Catholicism, I reasoned.

I had trouble finding anyone with whom I could sample Romania's finer cultural offerings. A day exploring the churches, mosques, and museums of the old town was all I got before our outings took a more mundane turn. Constanța had a resort district, replete with pristine beaches, bars, and clubs. Predictably, the swimwear customs of Romanian women were also a big draw for the Marines. I had a reputation as a religious man, and because I was Southern, my fellow Marines reimagined my Catholicism as an Evangelical-style preacher identity. They poked fun, but it didn't bother me. They also saw that I wasn't always the best Christian—fits of anger and swearing happen in the Corps, and I was not exempt.

It was quite exhilarating to wade into the Black Sea. Across this storied body of water lay Ukraine, Turkey, and Russia. These places I'd read about, almost like imaginary places, were so near at hand. I could feel the weight of history, of ages past, in the very air.

Russia soon became very important to us. All the turmoil of the past few years in Ukraine—we were across the Black Sea from it when it started, in 2014. We had been monitoring the US-backed overthrow of the Yanukovych government earlier in the year and the subsequent build-up of Russian forces on the border. We were shaken awake one morning to find those same Russian forces invading the Crimean Peninsula. We were put on high-alert, and spent the entire day and most of the night gathering and disseminating intelligence as it came in. We were basically the nearest American forces to the conflict zone, so there was a lot of hopeful excitement about us being on the frontline in a showdown with Russia (insane as that may sound). Luckily, the West backed down, and no Americans were sent in.

My actual encounter with Russia came in downtown Constanța. I was out with one of the counterintelligence operatives (the real James Bond, Secret Squirrel types), and we were in our civvies (non-military clothes). A raucous group of Russian sailors, in uniform, appeared down the street. When we met them mid-block, we hurriedly asked, like fanboys, if they would pose for pictures with us. With somewhat concerned looks on their faces and uneasy smiles, they agreed, their vanity perhaps getting the better of them. Next morning, our commander was treated to verified evidence of Russian troop presence in our AO with some up-close and personal IMINT of the enemy in his daily brief.

We were blessed to have a Catholic priest-chaplain on base, a saintly man originally from Ghana. Thankfully, most days my lunch schedule allowed me to attend daily Mass. This priest had a deep devotion to the Anima Christi prayer, and his quiet and peaceful manner impressed me. About midway through the deployment, a startling desire surfaced within me. I was drawing closer to God in prayer, and now thoughts of ordained priesthood started entering my mind. There was something powerfully attractive about them, too. But immediately came the rub: I was engaged to be married! And in love, right? I took the matter to the priest. To my surprise, he didn't try to talk me down or suggest that maybe I was just daydreaming. Rather, he gave credence to the possibility that this might be a genuine call from God. Such an answer disturbed and comforted me at the same time.

The first time I broke this development to my fiancée, we both broke down, and I eventually resolved to put the thought out of my mind. God wouldn't call me to hurt someone like this, and it was probably just a case of "grass is greener" anyway. But after I got back stateside, the nagging feeling didn't go away. I wrestled with it; I sought counsel from priests and married people; she and I fought over it. I dragged her to hell and back in the leadup to our wedding date in December.

With this type of back and forth, the emotionally mature thing to do would've been to break off the engagement or at least postpone the wedding. But passion and impatience, fear and impulsiveness all fed into this maelstrom. It came down to two or three weeks before the big day before I definitively called it off. Disgraceful, I know. But I was coming face to face with the ugly fragmentation in my own soul. There was a war within me, like St. Paul talks about (Romans 7:21–24). And that war deeply wounded another person. There were probably issues on both sides, and in the last analysis, I don't think either of us was ready for a binding life commitment of that kind, with all its duties and responsibilities, but that still doesn't excuse my dishonorable indecisiveness and cowardice. With heart still tottering, and barely self-impelled, I steered for seminary.

Non-Catholics would probably say, "See, this is the turmoil that occurs when you unnecessarily require celibacy of your clergy." And maybe, in a sex-saturated, anti-Catholic society, such a requirement *will* further suppress vocation numbers. But being married now, and having (sort of) lived in both headspaces, I can see the wisdom of the Church's requirement. First, naysayers have to reckon with the glorification of celibacy and virginity during the early centuries of the Church. Whether it was a requirement in some places or not for ordination, the whole thrust of the period was to hold it up as the ideal. And not just monastic celibacy, but celibacy in the world—consider all the consecrated virgins we commemorate in the Roman Canon every week. Priestly celibacy has been the most tangible way this emphasis, this spirit, has been preserved in the Western Church.

Second, priestly celibacy makes this much-needed corrective to the culture: not just material goods, but no, not even romance or family are the ultimate good, good as those things may be. God, and only God, is. This can be a great encouragement to all those who don't have these things—some people are, for whatever reason, unable to get married. Sometimes children don't come. But the celibate priest models and proclaims to everyone, "Undivided intimacy with God is the highest calling, and not only is it a necessary path for some, but I have *freely* chosen it—I have called God's bluff that he is enough, the all in all." This humbles and corrects the vision of married people. If they are tempted to place all their hopes in their spouse, or in their kids, they will soon be sorely disappointed. No imperfect human can withstand that kind of expectation. If your relationship (married or otherwise) is your greatest end, you will soon destroy it. And if you're like me, you'll then go tearing through relationship after relationship, looking for one that can bear your hopes, when none can. Relationship is an instrument God has provided to you to teach you love of others and of him. There's great fulfillment in it when lived toward that end, but not when lived as an end in and of itself. It, like all things, must be put in its place. Priestly celibacy dramatically does that.

So I broke the engagement. I got in touch with the Vocations Directors for both the Diocese of Nashville and the Archdiocese for the Military Services, and they got me into the co-sponsorship program, wherein they'd split the bill for my formation and training, and I'd serve out at least one contract as a military chaplain (of which there is a desperate shortage) before returning to Nashville as a parish priest. I had chosen God over all else, and we all lived happily ever after from then on, right?

In reality, the process was agonizing. What was I doing? Giving up the very real love of a flesh and blood woman for some pie-in-the-sky monk life? Who did I think I was? I could barely pass up a little butter at the supper table, much less give up romantic love and companionship for the rest of my life. And even though I'd known, for reasons other than my potential call to the priesthood, that marrying this girl was not the right thing to do, all I could remember now were the good times: the tenderness, the memories, the nicknames. I could barely walk through a place we'd gone together. Every song, every romantic movie—she was in them all. Her shade haunted my dreams and my nightmares. I had been purchased from slavery, and destined for freedom, but my wandering in the desert had only begun.

Quite literally, in fact. Though my contract would be converted into a direct commission as a Naval Officer in the late summer (the Marines use Navy chaplains), I spent the first three quarters of 2015 still living and training with my old unit. We got a slot at Twentynine Palms, California, where we were to run a lengthy desert maneuver training evolution. The locale was infamous in the Corps: hot as an oven and no civilization besides base itself for miles. We lived in stifling Quonset huts and took dust-choked rides on seven-ton trucks out into the desert. There we'd set up command and control tents and practice our field intelligence capabilities while the grunt platoons rode around in Ospreys. The intel work involved rotations throughout the night—a kind of email and sensor firewatch. Out here, in this unforgiving environment, I descended deeper into the trackless wasteland of my own inconstant heart. That line from antiquity started resonating in the back of my mind: those whom the gods would destroy they first drive mad.

Why had God driven me out here to die in this desert? Before this priesthood idea, I was going to pursue a career in the military or in intelligence with my devoted wife by my side. She was very attractive, and kind—who did I think I was, throwing her away like it was nothing? What kind of psychopath would devastate another person like that when he was just as attached as she was? What kind of masochist? Where were all those lofty spiritual lights and flighty consolations now, in this lonely place?

That was it: I had dynamited something real, tangible, and in the hand, for two doubtful birds in a bush that probably lived only in my imagination.

There was no shelter out here: I was exposed to the withering rays of my own passions. I was naked before them, with no distractions with which to cover myself. A miserable, scorched wreck, who'd wandered too far away from his fleshpots. I had to conclude that God had tricked me. He led me out into this desert only to desert me to the elements. Would that I were back in her embrace, with the old comforts. I had rather be a slave to them than a laughingstock out here.

One night, in the cramped comms tent, between the required checks I had to perform, I began crafting an email, addressed to her: I'm sorry; what was I thinking; take me back, I've learned my lesson; I'll never stray again; I was tricked, or something. As the wee hours drug on, I finetuned every line. It had to be perfect, and I had to be *committed* to it: were she to agree to try once more with me, and this evil madness overtake me a second time, would that a millstone be tied about my neck and I be cast into the sea before I hurt her again! I said a few pithy prayers for guidance, but I had made my decision. I was ripping this blindfold off and leaving this desert.

I looked over the email again, proofreading it for the tenth time. The end of my watch was approaching. I happened to refresh my inbox one more time, just out of habit. A new email appeared: Father Terrence McGowan. What in the world? I had emailed Father McGowan weeks ago, asking him for some kind of encouragement to stay on this seminary course despite my turmoil. I had received no answer—more silence from the One who led me out here, I supposed—until now? I opened the email. My eyes welled up as the contents became clear to me: *Dustin, this emotional confusion is not God's work. He wants to pull you through all this to the clarity of vocation that he's prepared for you. You're suffering from the effects of a disordered entanglement that is all so close in time to you that your emotions are still reeling from it. Discernment starts at seminary; it doesn't end there. The process of prioritizing your relationship with God above all else at seminary will allow you to see clearly. I am offering my Mass intentions for you. God bless you.*

I sat stunned. The email I'd composed to her hung in draft form in another window, awaiting some action. I deleted it. I lifted my eyes to the hanging ceiling of the tent and mouthed praise and thanks. What return could I make to this God, the Living God, who had shown his power once more, who had done for me what I couldn't do for myself? It was almost too incredible to believe, but he had saved me, unexpectedly, once again. He had allowed me to be tested to my absolute limit, but when my strength gave out, he had sent water from heaven to cool my tongue. The words from the man of God now bolstered me to stand erect, to forget my fears.

More than the words themselves was the dramatic and awe-inspiring way in which they'd been delivered, here at the eleventh hour. I told everyone. I told Carlos the next day, who usually rolled his eyes somewhat at my religious ravings, but even he was impressed. The madness hadn't left me, and wouldn't leave for some time, but I now had no doubt as to the right path. The pain therefore was not a sign that I should turn back but instead was the refiner's fire through which I must walk. My feet were on fire, walking across those blistering coals, but my resolve was now rendered unshakeable. Our time at Twentynine Palms came to an end, and soon I was stepping off the plane into the liquid atmosphere of coastal North Carolina, like a fish escaping back into its river.

With the help of some priest-chaplains in high places, I managed to get out of the Marine Corps and into the Navy Reserve in time for the beginning of the fall semester at seminary. Besides officer training in Rhode Island and check-ins with the local chaplain recruiter, my life would track completely with that of a regular Nashville seminarian. Bishop David Choby, of happy memory, was glad to have me on deck for my home diocese. He worked hard at recruiting serious men to the seminary during his bishopric, and the result has been a thriving diocese full of orthodox young priests. They had a great camaraderie, and I was privileged to become a part of it.

Chapter 9

The Household of God

At the time, Nashville sent most of its seminarians to the Pontifical College Josephinum in Columbus, Ohio. I was returning to the Midwest again—my former fiancée had been from there, and I'd gone there for Josh's wedding (he'd asked me and another Marine buddy to be in his wedding party). I was to live among the solid Midwestern Americans, for whom I've gained a lot of respect. The Josephinum was located in the northern suburbs of Columbus on what used to be the edge of town. It was a massive, Hogwarts-like edifice, filled with nooks and crannies and secret passages—lots of places that took on a different aspect after dark. I was enrolled in the Pre-Theology program, a two-year course of study that would culminate in another bachelor's degree, this one in philosophy. Four years of theology were required after that to reach priestly ordination.

Seminary was profoundly transformative. You're provided with an oasis in which to pray, study, and work with like-minded individuals. Seminary was where I was forced into philosophy, sometimes kicking and screaming (ahem, Aristotle), but it has since become one of my favorite subjects. Philosophy is a long, winding journey into the great questions of life and man's evolving answers. When once you've put in the hard work to learn and understand the twists and turns, you find that *to know* is truly a joy.

The friendships forged at seminary have proven to be some of the deepest and most lasting. It would be like if your Marine Corps buddies suddenly agreed with you on almost every controversial topic and had the same priorities. Probably chief among these fast friends was Curtis Weisenburger, from Putnam County, Ohio. Curtis is the only person with whom

I've had a heated, hours-long debate that ended in one of the parties saying, "Oh, okay. Well actually, that does make sense. I think you're right." (The debate was something about Socrates' suicide, and Curtis was the one who conceded, though he's bested me in several discussions since.) That was the thing about seminary—you could talk objectively about issues on which you disagreed such that no one got mad or went personal with it. This was the first time I'd been surrounded by people who enjoyed getting to the bottom of the big questions: religious, political, and philosophical. These types of discussions are not possible in the West at large today (if they ever were). If someone feels questioned or if talk has the potential to threaten someone's worldview, it's either strictly avoided or World War III erupts. People are incapable of bracketing a belief or idea and discussing it on its own merits anymore. I live off these kinds of discussions, though, so seminary was a paradise. I eventually married a woman who enjoys these types of conversations, thankfully.

We took a trip out to Putnam County and were hosted by Curtis's family at one point. There I found the type of small-town Americana I'd only seen in movies. Flat as a pancake and checkered by a quiltwork of wheat, soybean, and corn farms surrounding gridded little hamlets, the heavily German-settled county deeply impressed me. Most towns had a beautiful historic Catholic church, and the towns themselves were fairly well-maintained, with virtually no gawdy sprawl. Once you departed the city limits, you were in the domain of the farmer.

Curtis's dad was a former basketball coach at the town high school, and Curtis was a former player. He took us to a ballgame on Friday night, and I was floored by the passionate atmosphere of the heated rivalry. Each hamlet had its own high school, and so across the county there were extremely localized identities and loyalties. When Continental (Curtis's town) won the game, we flooded out onto Main Street and rolled the downtown, which was the victory tradition. I couldn't believe how idyllic it was: people had real devotion to the little places where they grew up and real fellow feeling for the people they grew up with.

Another unforgettable friend was Andrew Wisniewski, who was raised in Ohio but had roots in Philadelphia. Andrew had a pastor's heart and a prophet's sense of justice, so he defied political categories. Big Drew lifted weights and had experienced enough real life to temper his idealism, but he kept his passionate love for the poor and for what's right. He detested elitism in all its forms. Our conversations could go on for hours and through any number of disagreements. Never have I questioned the loyalty and sincerity of Andrew.

I also can't neglect to mention Robert Wagner, DDS. After decades of dentistry practice, Doc Bobby received some very pointed calls from God to go into the seminary. Despite being a bit more *seasoned* than most of our cohort, Rob fit like a hand in a glove, usually with more energy and optimism than anyone. Rob had the gift of gab, and his social ease and extroversion never ceased to amaze me.

Besides profoundly enduring friendships, seminary also gave me a love of wisdom—literally, philosophy. Being able to peel back the veil of life and events and observe the theoretical underpinnings has been one of the richest experiences of my life. For that reason, I love contemporary philosophy. I have a great sympathy for the postmodernists, strange as that may sound. The history of philosophy *is* the human story—it's the background to all the great movements.

Most importantly of all, though, is that seminary taught me how to pray. Seminary lays at your feet all the tools you need to enter into deep, prayerful communion with God: sacraments, books, instruction, peace, quiet, and time. As I said, my state of mind when I arrived was not altogether peaceful. I set about religiously (pun intended) devoting myself to a daily holy hour—I knew I needed God's nearness to navigate this swamp of conflicting emotions. I had never devoted myself to even ten minutes of prayer per day before this, at least not regularly. The effects were dramatic. I quickly discovered *lectio divina* as a surefire spur to prayerful meditation, that or some work of a saint or church father. I found that prayer truly was the path to communicating with God. He led me through intractable issues, gave me space for venting and mourning, and then showed me unending vistas of love, mercy, and peace. Though I am no adept at prayer, it was in the solitude of these many hours that I learned what truly mattered in life and gained the strength to begin pursuing it. Even as a beginner, it's clear to me that intimacy with God is all that matters. Seek that, and every other good thing will follow.

Let me emphasize, again, however, that I was only becoming acquainted with these realities. In no way had I mastered them. I was still wracked with guilt, indecision, and lack of trust. But prayer became like an oasis. Sometimes it was a knock-down, drag-out wrestling match with God-type of oasis—but then again, being completely demoralized and impoverished in spirit and confronting the Almighty with that is itself a form of healing.

So I worked out this relationship with trembling, and not a little fear, as I asked the question over and over: was I called to priesthood? As I learned from my spiritual director, I probably should've asked that question less frequently. Discernment many times takes the form of a dawning light rather than a light bulb. However, quite apart from the issue of whether or not I could or wanted to be celibate, I gradually became convinced that I didn't desire to *do* what a priest *does*. I didn't have any great passion for serving liturgy; I didn't enjoy teaching kids catechism; anointing the sick held no great allure for me. In short, none of the pastoral aspects of the job, which are arguably the most important parts, appealed to me. I wanted to be close to God, but I didn't want to be a priest, in the final analysis. Seminary gave me the tools to distinguish those two things.

I nearly left after the first year, but after taking counsel, including with the diocesan vocations director, I decided to stay, to let things even out and to really make sure. And that second year was pure gift. I was more settled, more present. I fully let go of my former fiancée and studied, worked, and prayed in that great Flemish Gothic castle on High Street.

It became clear that my first intimations were correct, and that I would need to make a plan for what to do once I left seminary. I decided to return to my original career path, urban planning. I would need a master's degree to get very far, though. I successfully applied for a summer internship with the state transportation department back home and for the University of Memphis's master's program in City and Regional Planning that was due to start that fall. I suspected I was called to marriage, and I wanted to pursue something that lent itself to stability and local involvement. Plus, I intuited the deep impact the built environment has on all of us, and I wanted to shape it for the better.

I moved in with my old friend Mark for the summer. But a new question had begun to burrow into my mind—one that threatened the entire social and mental world I'd built so far. It's a fair question to ask—what's left? Does all this searching ever end? One last possibility hadn't been tested, however.

While in seminary, I'd picked up an aid to prayer by a Swiss Benedictine monk, Gabriel Bunge, OSB.[1] In it Father Bunge gives a tour of the theology and praxis of Evagrius Ponticus, an ascetical writer of the fourth century who collated the ideas, traditions, and practices of the

---

1. Bunge. *Earthen Vessels.*

wider Egyptian monastic movement. What I read astounded me. There were actually prescribed "best practices," so to speak, for how to pray, and I hadn't been taught them. For one thing, standing was the normal prayer posture—kneeling was only for penance or extreme supplication. Kneeling wasn't even allowed in the ancient churches from Easter until Pentecost because of its penitential character, that season being one of joy and triumph. It was also important which way you faced: always find east, and set your face in that direction, with hands upheld. Too, there was symbolism behind the direction in which a Christian was to perform the sign of the cross—right to left, not the other way around—exactly the opposite of what we Catholics did.

I found that following some of these rules did enhance my prayer somewhat, and also helped explain why sitting during prayer had generally felt inappropriate to me. The church fathers taught that posture was very important in determining the quality of prayer. This principle made sense to me—after all, as Catholics we certainly believed in an embodied spirituality. That was the whole idea behind sacraments.

But it irked me that we had seemingly strayed from the recommendations of the earliest Christians. I was further irked to learn that Father Bunge—obviously a holy man, from every indication I could see—had eventually converted to Eastern Orthodox Christianity. Wasn't that just Catholicism for Greeks and Russians? That's why I had dismissed it when I was weighing the various Christian options, years ago. Maybe I should've given it a closer look?

Another spiritual book I'd loved in seminary was *The Ladder of Divine Ascent*, by St. John Climacus. This book was written in the seventh century, well before the Great Schism between East and West, but it's much more popular within Eastern Orthodoxy, and the spirit and style are certainly of the East. The rigorously ascetical spirituality found within it appealed to the extremist in me and seemed essential to living a healthy celibate life. I hadn't explicitly seen that commitment to discipline in all things at seminary, and it worried me. Would I have been prepared to live that kind of life?

I had also seen what I thought was an important difference between Eastern and Western (i.e., Roman Catholic) spirituality. Were these just different styles? Or were there substantive differences involved? I started perusing Eastern Orthodox apologetic websites and books. I was surprised to learn that, from their perspective at least, these were crucial, church-splitting differences. The Filioque was the main one: the dogma, held in the

West, that the Holy Spirit proceeds from both the Father and the Son. The East maintains this is a harmful innovation that even distorts the central Christian dogma of the Trinity. Separate but related is the idea of Absolute Divine Simplicity (ADS). The Orthodox claim that Catholics are bound by their post-schism councils to hold that the Divine Essence is absolutely simple, an idea purportedly more from Aristotle than from Scripture and Tradition. Maybe most importantly, the East charges that we're all ultramontanists in the West, or that we give the Roman Pope outsized, if not idolatrous, importance relative to the rest of the church and its governance.

But far above and beyond all these somewhat obscure considerations was the lived experience of Orthodoxy, chiefly in the liturgy. If you've spent any time in the Catholic world, you know there's something called the "liturgy wars" raging—and it's been raging since the Novus Ordo version of the Mass was imposed on the Church in 1970. At that time, a simplified version of the central experience of Catholic worship was made mandatory, all at once. In its essentials, it is faithful to what the Mass has always been—it's undoubtedly "valid," as every necessary part is still present. Yet the missal it came with stripped (or allowed the stripping of) all the familiarity out of the externals: the ancient settings and chants, even the direction the priest faced: everything was made optional. This is to the point where a Novus Ordo Mass could be celebrated to be almost indistinguishable from a Traditional Latin Mass (to the untrained eye), *or* it could be "performed" with guitars, dancing, clowns, you name it. Even where the bastardization is not this egregious, the vast majority of Novus Ordo Masses feature off-the-cuff wisecracks from Father Dave, armies of lay extraordinary Eucharistic Ministers swarming the altar, and the most saccharine, cheeseball soccer-mom worship "hymns" you can imagine. It has driven men (and most people with even an inkling of a sense of the sacred) from Mass attendance in droves and completely alienated Millennials and Zoomers (who somehow still have an appetite for mystery and transcendence).

This situation can seem tolerable to a serious young Catholic because there are exceptions, such as the TLM itself (though its very existence is currently in danger) or a reverent Novus Ordo (few and far between though they may be). That is, until you learn about Eastern Orthodoxy. Go to any Orthodox parish, of whatever ethnic jurisdiction, and you'll find liturgy, chant, and hymns virtually untouched by the wrongheaded tinkering that has become endemic in the Catholic Church. Depending on the skill level and resources of the parish, it can be breathtaking, but it's always at least appropriate for the worship of God. Related but separate is the issue of fasting. The Orthodox do it constantly, which is how the early Church did it. How often are Roman Catholics supposed to fast? From even just sixty or so years ago, when we at least fasted for all of Lent and before major solemnities, the required fasting days have been reduced to a sum total of *two*—two days, out of three-hundred and sixty-five. Surely speaking of a wholesale abandonment of fasting in the West is not hyperbole.

As I learned of the experiential, tangible differences between the communions, I couldn't help but go see for myself. I began attending Mass on Saturday evenings at various Catholic Churches to fulfill my obligation, with my disgust growing at the near universal banality I witnessed, and then attending the Orthodox Divine Liturgy on Sunday mornings as an observer. I reconnected with an Orthodox priest I'd met years before while working at Kroger and picked his brain about these issues. I moved to Memphis for grad school but drove back and forth to Nashville on the weekends to see my then-girlfriend. I reached out to Father Terry Johnston, a convert himself, who was starting a Western Rite Orthodox parish in Nashville. Father Terry was one of the truest pastors of souls I'd ever met: humble, self-sacrificing, and truly concerned about the welfare of his flock and his friends. The aforementioned priest from my past was the same way (Father Parthenios Turner, still a dear friend). These men, though married, gave of themselves and their time to overflowing.

The services I witnessed affected me deeply. The whole congregation joined in, producing exquisite harmonies. The churches were uniformly beautiful, usually decked out with Byzantine-style icons. And as I read more Orthodox sources, I discovered that the currents in Eastern spirituality I'd probed in seminary were, according to the Orthodox, not just flavors of the same faith, but church-dividing distinctives. Western theology, according to this view, was penal substitutionary (i.e., focused on paying back the debt of sin) and legalistic. It led to neuroses and despair. Eastern theology, on the other hand, was therapeutic, healing, medicinal, and not rigid or overly concerned with rules. It was the West's differences with the East, they maintained, that led to Protestantism and the slide into atheistic secularism. No such devolution had occurred in Orthodox lands!

Before I knew what had happened, I was somehow staring another conversion process in the face. Leave the Catholic Church? The loving mother I'd found nearly a decade before? The mother who'd ushered me to the Eucharistic table and sacramental union with Christ? Well, she hadn't been a great mother as of late, it seemed. And if Orthodoxy was true, then her faults meant she wasn't my mother at all, but an impostor.

The potential embarrassment of changing my religion yet again was balanced, however, by a dangerous but tantalizing possibility. As expected, my family had been actively shunning me in the years since I'd left for Parris Island that fateful morning. I'd been able to drop in a few times in order to get my stuff, but these visits lasted no more than fifteen minutes usually. They were always awkward, and sometimes tense. Momma looked haggard and depressed; Daddy stoic and unmoved. The situation for some reason didn't bother me as much then as it does now, yet the pain was still something I was desperately seeking to end, in any way except apostasy from my faith . . . but what if my faith were to change? What if, in that space between the former faith and the new faith—in the time where I technically had no settled faith—I could go to the Witnesses and say the bare minimum necessary to get reinstated, and then just neglect to tell them later when I joined the Orthodox Church? I had good reason to believe they were hurting as much as I was despite their intransigence. Was there not some way, then? I consulted with an Orthodox priest in Lexington, Kentucky. He listened to my plan but said he'd have to pray on it. There were many things, even as a potentially "unchurched" Christian, that I would be unable to say to the JW authorities. Would noncommittal answers and vacillations be enough? Would they ask me to renounce the Trinity, for example?

In the last analysis, it was impossible. There was too much deception involved, too many risks of betraying Christ. And even if it were to succeed, it would require erasing any public expression of my faith from then on—one stray picture of a Christmas tree on social media could instantly bring the whole charade crashing down. And of course I'd be getting married in an Orthodox or Catholic church, God willing—how would I explain that? The only way to "fade" from the Witness organization and avoid the shunning punishment is to ever after hide your beliefs in a closet. I believe this is why many ex-JWs drift into nihilism and never seek religious community again.

Regardless, the moment of truth concerning the East had come. Father Terry asked me on the phone one night: are you ready to become a catechumen? I'd moved into the upstairs bedroom of a house in Midtown Memphis. I lived a Spartan existence, with nothing but my clothes folded on a shelf and a foam pallet on the floor for my bed. "You're past ready," he said to me. I could tell he was eager and excited for my journey in faith.

I hesitated. "Not yet," I said, sitting on the floor of my room, back leaned against the wall. "I've got to make sure. This is a huge decision."

I got a book by an English Catholic priest written in the early twentieth century as a polemic against the Anglican Church.[2] Tellingly, many of the arguments I was hearing from the Orthodox against the Catholics were straight out of earlier Anglican controversialist literature. All these arguments from the church fathers I'd read from the Orthodox seemed airtight, but this priest at least had a reply to each of them. It turns out that there's an equally plausible Catholic or Orthodox spin one can put on any of these historical events. The Orthodox point out that Nicaea places Rome on a level with Antioch and Alexandria, but then an early church historian like Sozomen says nothing should be done without Rome's consent. There's an Orthodox- and conciliarist-sounding Fifth Ecumenical Council right before a Catholic- and papalist-sounding Sixth.[3]

I came away concluding that the historical evidence, at least, was inconclusive. Some churchmen acted at times like the Pope was the Supreme Pontiff and others at other times treated him more like a first among equals. But at least this priest's book had shown me that the case for Orthodoxy was not as open and shut as it seemed at first glance.

So history and the councils seemed mixed in their testimony—what about theology? The most penetrating criticism by the best Orthodox apologists is not about the Filioque or the Papacy, believe it or not. It's instead centered around the little-known topic of divine simplicity. Neither side doubts that God's essence is supposed to be simple. The question is whether it is "absolutely" simple. The Orthodox say that the West, for reasons of language, culture, and the supposed loss of much of our philosophical and theological heritage during the Dark Ages, adopted the Aristotelian view that God is *absolutely* simple. (Apparently, this gave us fits when trying to understand how an absolutely simple essence could exist in three persons or even create freely and *ex nihilo*, since persons would introduce diversity into the Godhead, and a world that didn't always exist and could've *not* existed would introduce a "before and after," and therefore contingency, into an essence that was supposed to exist eternally unchanged and unchanging.) The Orthodox pointed to the documents of Vatican I as dogmatizing this

---

2. Fortescue, *Early Papacy*.

3. This is notwithstanding Pope Honorius's condemnation at the same council, but even that must be balanced with the stunning deference given to Pope Hormisdas a couple hundred years prior.

belief to show that Roman Catholics must believe this purportedly pagan conception. Their position is that God encompasses an unapproachable, incomprehensible essence on the one hand and "energies" on the other, which "come down to us" and constitute our experience of God. These would be like God's love, his foresight, his justice, etc. The personal "divisions" implicit in the dogma of the Trinity seem less problematic for this model.[4]

The ultimate conclusion of all these minute wrong turns in the West was the scholastic rationalism that occluded the lived experience of God and resulted in Protestantism, secularism, atheism, and nihilism.

They had a point. Why did things go so wrong in the West? Why did we change so many things? Was it because we'd been groping around in the darkness caused by our loss of the lived experience of the Divine Energies? There are knock-on effects of this loss, according to them. The East kept alive the austere, mystical spirituality of the first millennium fathers. In the West, we devolved into the aforementioned rationalism of the scholastics, the morbidity of the stigmatists, and the saccharine delusions of the young women saints. And hadn't I perceived something like this in my attraction to the Eastern Fathers?

I set about testing this claim next as I'd tested the historical one. Once again, I wanted the Orthodox critique to be true, sad to say. I wanted another escape to a better, purer Christianity, one that would allow me to wash my hands of everything that had begun to disillusion me within Catholicism. I started reading both Western and Eastern saints. I wanted to peer beneath the stylistic differences. First, was the East a land of light and resurrection while the West was all dejected obsession with the crucifixion and suffering? Was the "dark night of the soul," made so famous by Saint John of the Cross, part of the necessary path to God or just the sad and unnecessary result of the impoverished state of Western spirituality cut off by "absolute" simplicity from the energies of God?

I found a doctoral dissertation online by an Orthodox academic that meant to investigate this question by comparing and contrasting Saint John of the Cross with Saint Symeon the New Theologian, a prominent Eastern saint from the end of the first millennium known for his joyful and luminous spiritual teaching.[5] From the abstract and the title, I felt that surely this "deep dive" would provide the substantial proof necessary to corroborate

---

4. I refer you to my friend Dr. David Bradshaw's landmark book-length study on this issue for a complete understanding: *Aristotle East and West*.

5. Pulkkanen. "Dark Night."

the sweeping dismissals of Western spirituality that I'd encountered in the Orthodox polemicists.

I read the entire book-length document, replete with extensive quotes and passages from both saints. The stages of spiritual growth were laid out according to each saint, including the "dark nights" of St. John. Interestingly, though, St. Symeon also described painful "purgative" stages in which violence against the passions and even against the desire for spiritual delights (much akin to St. John's dark night of the soul) were necessary. And also tellingly, St. John describes an eventual arrival at a peaceful, mystically oriented state much like that of St. Symeon—St. John's "infused contemplation." The end of the dissertation came, and the hoped for striking contrast between East and West had failed to materialize.

I spoke on the phone with Father Terry about all this. "You have to understand," I explained. "The history, the obscure theological disagreements—I for one will *never* be able to base a decision to leave something as consequential and unignorable as the Roman Catholic Church based on these. My conclusion about the historicity of papal supremacy or the essence/energies distinction can literally change based on my mood or which Church Father I've read most recently. And I think anyone who says differently is either a world-class scholar with loads more time, energy, and brainpower than me or is just elaborately trying to confirm his own bias, which I've somehow failed to do. Therefore," I continued, "I had to base my decision on the practical, consequential impacts of the communions in question—their teachings on how we encounter God and how we are to live. If Orthodox teaching and practice really provided something Catholicism has lost, then to me that's the best evidence. But that's not what I found, and so I'm not going to put my salvation in jeopardy (because rending the Body of Christ unnecessarily would probably do that) just because I 'prefer' Eastern spirituality. Even if I did, I'd certainly stay Catholic, since Rome offers Eastern rites and churches as options!"

"I think I just pushed too hard, too fast," Father Terry said.

"No, Father; if it was simply a matter of what you've done, I would've become Orthodox a long time ago. You've been one of the greatest examples of Christian priesthood I've ever encountered. But unless Catholicism was manifestly wrong, I couldn't leave it. And I've done enough looking into it at this point to conclude that there are not church-dividing differences when it comes to spiritual practice and theory. The saints of the West are not delusional." I was staying Catholic.

Chapter 10

Under the Sign of the Cross

Father Terry didn't press the issue (he and I have remained friends), but perhaps he should have, after all the other issues with Catholicism I've raised. While the arguments over the exact nature of the Godhead and the alleged differences in the saints and their spiritualities may not warrant jumping ship, the impoverished nature of Catholic parish and liturgical life compared to Orthodoxy might seem to justify it. Wouldn't that be proof enough that Rome has fallen? Irreverent masses and virtually nonexistent fasting?

To these accusations I have but one defense. It is not, as many Catholic apologists do, to try to soften the blow of the charges. I can't run from the gravity of these problems and bury my head in the sand. It would eat away at me. Rather, I believe most sincerely that we are in the midst of one of those world-historic crisis periods that have plagued the church of Christ from time to time since her founding.

One benefit of diving into the fathers and the early councils is that you get to see how many times throughout history that the church has been similarly submerged in controversy. Perhaps the most instructive such controversy was the first one: the great Arian crisis of the fourth century. It is somewhat well-known that Saint Constantine the Great convoked the first Ecumenical Council in Nicaea to settle the issue. It's less well-known that even after he did so, the controversy raged incessantly for half a century longer, with nearly every bishop capitulating to the Arian philosophy in some form or fashion. It occasioned even a failure by the reigning Pope, Liberius, to clearly enunciate the truth in the face of persecution.

Looking at that sad spectacle, one may duly ask: so the central dogma of Christianity (the divinity of Christ and the triune nature of God) was sufficiently unclear to the first post-catacombs generation of Christians that most of the leadership and some portion of the faithful were willing to jettison it, modify it, or at least waffle on it based on temporal inducements? Yes, history clearly demonstrates that this was so. If that could've happened so early in her history, then where do we get off asserting that the current crisis should be impossible in the true church, and that therefore Rome was never that church to begin with? The situation is strikingly analogous: a seductive distortion of the faith (modernism) sweeps the church, dragging many of the bishops and even certain popes (notwithstanding their *ex cathedra* pronouncements and official magisterium) down with it. Discipline collapses (leading to the abuse crisis), wrongheaded ideas gain currency (leading to the liturgical and fasting crises), and churchmen sycophantically worship the powers that be (bishops supporting every fashionable cause or project and refusing to speak truth to power).

As with the Arian crisis, no definitive, magisterial declaration of heresy has been promulgated or approved. For whatever vagueness it may contain, Vatican II does not reverse any established dogma or doctrine. It may represent an unfortunate change of emphasis or voice that has had mixed results, but that's not heresy. Keep in mind that several Ecumenical Councils have led to schisms (e.g., the fourth) and some that were convened to heal them (e.g., the fifth) failed to do so, so admitting the policy missteps of a council is not "questioning the Holy Spirit's guidance of the church" or something like that. The ultimate purpose of any council in God's providence is not always clear, and Vatican II may indeed one day bear fruit in the way most of its authors intended.

During Arianism, the many mealy-mouthed regional councils and even the statement of faith signed by Pope Liberius under pressure were not infallible, and neither are the rapidly multiplying declarations, agreements, exhortations, and airplane interviews of the current occupants of the church's highest echelons. The church knows how to pronounce definitively on a topic. She has the tools at hand. She has manifestly *not* done that on the currently contested topics because if she were intending to "reverse" some previously settled question, the level of clarity required would arguably be even greater than normal. For all the disheartening bluster, pandering, and silence of many prelates, in the long run, all this really won't amount to a hill of beans.

So that's step one for remaining Catholic: making your peace with the current level of dysfunction by realizing that we are indeed living through one of those signal church-rocking waves of insanity that Satan inflicts and God permits every couple hundred years. You don't have to be okay with clown or rock band masses. You don't have to endorse the radical political priorities of some bishops. You don't have to try to contort every word the Holy Father says into some restatement of orthodoxy. These things are all problems, and we need to acknowledge them as such, but they are not causes for despair. They're the prelude to a glorious return to the fullness of Catholic life and teaching by some future generation; or, we're on the doorstep of the eschaton. Either way.

In fact, experiencing these periodic upheavals is much more in line with the experience of the historic church and really proves our identity with the same. During the fourth century, chances are, your bishop probably would've disbelieved in the full divinity of Christ. In the fifteenth century, your bishop probably would've been a worldly prince who abused indulgences. And during the twenty-first century, your bishop probably talks incessantly about dialogue and unlimited immigration and makes wisecracks during the Holy Liturgy. Welcome to the fallen world. The Church in her mystical reality and in the teachings she officially holds and defends as teacher and mother remains spotless and pure. But everything else is more or less up to human freedom and depends on our faithfulness, and on many things outside our control besides. Heretical controversies are the problem of evil applied to the church. Evil doesn't disprove God, and human faithlessness and failings don't disprove the church. If the Magisterium is intact (and it is), then Christ's promise has not failed. The pure standard is still held aloft, still there for all the world to see if they are willing to look.

As an example, just ask yourself: what does the Catholic Church teach about artificial birth control? Despite the fact that few want to preach this anymore, the church still teaches that it's intrinsically—that is, everywhere and always—immoral. That's still on the books, and will remain so. Only divine intervention could have kept such an ignored and unpopular teaching around!

And that brings me to three positive reasons for remaining a Catholic. The first is that intact teaching on the immorality of artificial contraception. The entire civilized world shared this belief until the twentieth century. It's not in question that historic Christianity and the fathers rejected contraception either, which is another reason this teaching is such an important demarcation line. Literally ever other major Christian body has capitulated on this issue, worldwide Orthodoxy (even the Moscow Patriarchate) included. Usually so exactingly scrupulous about adhering to the praxis of the first millennium church, the Orthodox have inexplicably dropped the ball on this one.

Their defense goes, "The Church Fathers denigrate intentionally non-procreative sex of any type. For them, only sex that was intended to beget offspring is morally praiseworthy. Therefore, since you Catholics allow natural family planning (NFP), or the timing of the sexual act so as to avoid pregnancy, you too have strayed from the fathers and are in the same boat as we are (who allow artificial barrier methods at least, if not worse things like the pill)." On the face of it, this is an absurd argument. It says, in effect, "Yeah, we changed and abandoned the common heritage—but you did too in a lesser way, and so you have no room to talk." Or, "Yeah, but look what you did!" It's clear that the Catholic position would at least be closer to the fathers here, which ought to count for something for those looking for the historic church.

Granted, I accept that many fathers speak as if all intentionally non-procreative sex is wrong. But it's important to note that St. Augustine, who is oft derided (and not entirely without reason) as the most negative of all the fathers toward sex, classes lying with one's wife for a reason other than the desire to beget offspring as only a venial sin. It was obviously not, then, considered the type of moral abomination that onanism was. And there's a very big difference between choosing not to do something, such as refraining from sex during a fertile period, and choosing to actively obstruct the purpose of the act, even if the end result, no conception, is the same.

It's true that NFP can be abused. There needs to be a just reason for using it to avoid conception. Catholics have taken the Orthodox insistence on conscience and discernment regarding this issue and merely applied it to the decision of whether to use NFP or not, rather than applying it to the decision of whether or not to use artificial contraception. Catholic moral theology does not permit relying on your conscience when it comes to intrinsically evil acts. To reserve the total self-gift is never permissible. The act itself is disordered. However, fully natural marital relations are by nature morally licit between spouses. The potential for wrongdoing therefore doesn't attach to the act considered in a vacuum (as it does to contraceptive sex), but to the circumstances in which the act is performed, or the motives involved. We Catholics do allow room for personal judgment, conscience, and consultation with a spiritual father regarding child-bearing decisions. However, we don't allow such considerations to make things that are wrong in and of themselves good. But then, it seems this is another fundamental difference between the communions.

Practically and emotionally speaking, I was convinced of the truth of this teaching the first time I stepped foot into a traditional Catholic parish. Families of five, six, seven, even ten children turned the coffee hour after Mass into an explosion of life. That's what I saw there: life. Most Americans under age ninety have probably never experienced anything like it because birth rates in this country have been falling for around a hundred years now. We decided long ago, under pressure from Malthusian elites, that both humanity's happiness and survival somehow depended on there being fewer of us around. That's not only a lie scientifically; it turns out that human life, human flourishing, increases when there are more humans. When a couple's love overflows with gratuitous self-gift, new eternal souls freely come into existence as a result and enrich the world (and the economy) around them.

That's one of the most lamentable attitudes that's seeped into every Christian organization, except for the church and those who follow it: this reflexive, hackneyed assumption that anyone in their right mind would never have more than two, or at the absolute most, three, children. Start talking about a fourth, and the groans and mouthed exclamations start rolling in. It's not even considered rude. There's no awareness that outside this narrow hundred-year slice of history, mankind has universally regarded a large family as not only a blessing, but even a necessary condition for the good life.

Sure, some of that was purely economic (big farms require many hands), but experiencing large families firsthand has convinced me that it's spiritual as well. Their absence is the gaping hole in our common life in the West. It's the missing piece from which all our sexual dysfunction flows. And it's the path of sanctification and maturation that so many of us are missing.

The second reason for remaining a Catholic is more tenuous, but still, I'd wager, something to hang your hat on. That's the teaching on divorce and remarriage. The teaching is that a valid sacramental marriage is indissoluble, meaning that not only is remarriage after divorce not permitted if both spouses are still alive—it's not even possible. The Orthodox have been allowing up to three marriages (but with a penitential ceremony for the second and third) for at least a thousand years, and there's evidence it goes back further than that. I'm not arguing with that.

What I'm saying is that the Western and Catholic practice surely gets more at the heart of Christ's teaching on marriage, and once again it's alone in the world in insisting on this rigor. Really, what is marriage if it's not indissoluble? It would be nothing, a mere convenience. There has to be no way out except death, or the analogy of Christ and the church makes no sense (Ephesians 5:22–33). If a man can dismiss an adulterous woman (or vice versa), then the Protestants are right: let Christ espouse the new, reformed bride and put away this Roman harlot. And likewise with the new bride, as each communion grows haughty and strays.

And no, annulments are not the same. Of course I have a personal stake in this debate, but I really do believe that if our exalted, exacting view of marriage is true, many modern-day marriages in no way rise to that bar. When I entered my civil marriage, I did not believe it was an irreversible decision. Neither did I believe we needed to be open to life. What I was "doing" with my "I do" wasn't the same thing Catholics do.

The agitation against this teaching seemed to find some official support in Pope Francis's *Amoris Laetitia* exhortation.[1] Did this document indeed allow divorce and remarriage? I can't say. Burying a stunning reversal of previously crystal-clear doctrine in a vague footnote doesn't sound like a magisterial pronouncement to me. Until I'm clearly told otherwise, I'll continue to see this beautiful and forceful revelation of the permanence of marriage as another evidence for Catholicism.[2]

The final, and for me, most convincing reason to be a Catholic is also the simplest and most undeniable. It's only this: the Roman Catholic Church is the biggest, most universal, and most authoritative apostolic church on earth. It is the largest single religion, encompassing over one-seventh of the world's population. It is the only universal faith: it has a substantial, independent presence in every major region and people group on the globe (i.e., there are "Catholic countries" in Europe, Asia, the Americas, and Africa). It is the exclusive provenance of no one people or language group. And it's also the one that matters most. No one's too heartbroken or surprised when

---

1. Pope Francis. "*Amoris Laetitia.*"

2. The same goes for any of the supposed changes in Catholic doctrine and practice in recent years. A Catholic must interpret whatever is unclear or seemingly contradictory in light of the clear and established tradition of the church, quite apart from any suspicions he may have about the motivations behind such statements. What else could he be expected to do?

this or that Protestant denomination capitulates on the hot button issue of the hour. But if Rome were to fall on some non-negotiable, everyone would take notice: it would mean something.

I can hear the Orthodox now: "Triumphalism! Truth is not determined by a show of hands! Your dominance is due to evil colonialism! And besides, in the Bible, it was the smaller two-tribe kingdom of Judah that remained God's people, not the larger ten-tribe kingdom of Israel!"

Here's the thing, though: the true God is the lord of history. Read the Old Testament. God's will, his purposes, are accomplished by the very ordinary hands of men across the unfolding of the ages. Rewards, punishments—God doles them out sometimes in very roundabout ways, it's true, but still in ways that ultimately accomplish his designs. So when the prophecies speak of a worldwide ingathering of the New Israel, of ten men grabbing 'holt of the skirt of a Jew, of a pure sacrifice being offered from the rising of the sun to its setting—these are guarantees from God that the Kingdom of the Messiah will not be a localized, ethnic, inconsequential phenomenon.

So you have to ask yourself: is it possible that God would allow an ancient organization founded by the Messiah, which subsequently over the course of its history fulfilled all of these prophecies, to actually be an anti-Christian counterfeit? Surely, this would be one of the greatest bait-and-switches of all time. If it was, you'd have to conclude, with the original Reformers, that Rome is not just a wayward church, but rather the abomination of desolation itself. The Antichrist. But who, beyond a few unhinged street preachers, can maintain that with a straight face? Not to excuse the many sins of some clergy or Church members generally, but an honest assessment reveals that these faults are no more numerous or egregious than those of other bureaucratic bodies. And what of her saints? Could the Mother of Mother Teresa be the mistress of Satan? Yes, the infernal one dolls himself up as an angel of light, but going too far down that rabbit hole leads to crippling paranoia and an inability to decipher reality. Madness that way lies. The bare fact, which everybody knows, is that there's *one* universal society of Christians spread throughout the world. It's the only communion that could credibly bear the name "catholic," which comes from a Greek word meaning "of the whole" (and thus even its detractors are forced to admit its unique position every time they name it).

It's not a case of, "Oh, 1.2 billion Catholics vs. 300 million Eastern Orthodox;[3] therefore, Catholicism is true." It's how the lord of history could permit the Antichrist to so uniquely embody the markers that only his one, holy, and apostolic church was foretold to possess. It would be a joke so cruel, so confusing, that it would almost call into question his command that all men join his visible body. And what of the colonialism charge? Do we hear similar criticisms of Constantine and the Roman Empire's role in advancing Christianity in the first millennium? No, because adherents of any ideology or belief system are generally glad to see its spread and promotion by those in power, full stop. This goes for first millennium Christianity, second millennium western Christianity, Enlightenment rationalism, socialism, civil rights, and democracy. Only a small coterie of "principled" "conservatives" in our day and age who have fetishized "losing with dignity" decry such methods. But I think the Iraq War of the last few decades proves that even they can be persuaded. Even if we were to grant colonialism as an unqualified evil, that does not mean God couldn't have used it to accomplish his purpose of gathering in his church.

The final counter-argument from the Eastern Orthodox I cited above is probably the most effective: the example of God in the Bible choosing the smaller Judah over the larger Israel as his people. Of course that's true, but then again the prophecies relating to the worldwide spread of the New Israel didn't apply to the old Israel. Nothing prevented such an arrangement from occurring in the lead up to the birth of the savior. Ancient Israel, and then the Jews, were by definition a special people limited in number and dispersion. By the nature of things they were a very particular people, smaller than most nations, and so it's not surprising that the smaller faction of Abraham's descendants ultimately carried the day. A particular people birthed a particular man, whose Kingdom was to be universal. As

---

3. Or 60 million. I've never understood why, if we're open to the idea of the less universal Greek-Russian Eastern Orthodox Church being the one true church, that we wouldn't also extend that possibility to the Oriental Orthodox Church (the ancient Christian communion that encompasses the Churches of Egypt, Ethiopia, Armenia, and large segments of Syrian and Indian Christianity, among others). That communion encompasses roughly the same number of "people groups" that the Eastern Orthodox do; to wit: The oriental church's Africans, Egyptians, Middle Easterners (to paint with a broad brush), Caucasians (Armenians) and Indians; versus the eastern church's Greeks, Slavs, Middle Easterners, Romanians, and Caucasians (Georgians). If numbers and dispersion don't matter, then what makes their claim less legitimate? Why should we believe recognizing seven Ecumenical Councils makes more sense than only recognizing three?

the advance guard of that Kingdom, the church was prophesied to be, and manifestly has become, universal, as well.

So all the caveats and nuances of the historical, theological, and moral arguments being what they are (and being in a practical sense intractable to all but the most committed scholars, who even so disagree), the one brute, bare, and indisputable fact that the great majority of humanity is forced to concede no matter their persuasion or worldview is that the Roman Catholic Church is the only church whose teachings, lineage, and dispersion around the world and across cultures allow it to credibly claim to be the universal society of the Gospel, if we take the prophecies regarding the church in the Old Testament literally. This is a fact accessible to everyone and anyone. It requires no esoteric knowledge of church history, conciliar documents, or theology. It's the kind of all-too-obvious evidence you would expect from the God of public revelation if he wanted there to be one obvious standard to which all men should flock.

The Catholic Church forces the evangelical decision that Christ himself forces, as detailed by C.S. Lewis. "Who do you say that I am?"[4] Your answer to that question, once you accept the veracity of the Gospel accounts, is Lord, liar, or lunatic. There's no "good man but a bit mistaken on his identity" option. Anyone claiming what Christ claimed, and not being it, would be either crazy or evil. Likewise with his church. The early Reformers were right: if this massive, overpowering fact is not *the* church, then it must be *the* whore of Babylon. Its claims for itself leave us no other option. Many bold Orthodox have concluded similarly, while stopping short of directly using that language. Ask yourself: is it truly reasonable to side with these broken and factious fragments against the great fact of the *oneness* of the Catholic Church?

But look at how corrupt she is! Surely this may finally be her undoing, if prophecy and theology fail us. Two things: the first is somewhat weak, but it's relevant nonetheless. The Catholic Church is no more corrupt than any other bureaucratic organization. It may seem that way from the inordinate amount of attention her misdeeds get in the media, but a closer look will reveal all the same scandals among the Baptists, the Orthodox, the Jehovah's Witnesses, the Boy Scouts, and even the public school teachers. She is clearly the largest single such organization, and of course the corruption of the best is the worst. But the idea in many minds that she is some singular example of malfeasance is just not true.

4. Lewis, *Mere Christianity*, 52.

Now, that's not to excuse what evil she has tolerated, hidden, and even fostered at times. For these crimes, as St. John Chrysostom vividly describes, the skulls of those responsible surely line the pathways into Hell. I'm confident there is no shortage of millstones waiting in the next world for a great many of us. And you could fairly argue that God's one true church should be above the mean average of dysfunction in the world, not level with it. But aside from the fact that Christ predicted it would be so—the wheat and the chaff would share a barn until his Second Coming, after all (Matthew 13:24–30)—her dysfunction is really nothing more than the problem of evil applied to the church.

The problem of evil, again, is the philosophical difficulty of squaring an all-good and all-powerful God with the existence of evil. Evil implies that God is either not all good or not all powerful; else he would not allow its existence. The Christian answer to this conundrum is the preeminence of love in God's universe, a precondition of which is free will. Love requires freedom, so any reality where love is the goal must feature the potential for evil, at least in some form or fashion. The choice of evil will either not exist or be so discredited as to *functionally* not exist in the Eschaton, where God will be all in all, but it certainly exists at every level of our world now, including in the church. Great graces to avoid evil are offered in the church, but great sin is possible if—especially if—those graces are rejected.

And so while the headlines are certainly full of the weeds, consider how great the wheat is! In her saints the church *does* rise above the level of every other organization, including the best they have to offer. Her philanthropy and charity are also unrivalled. So perhaps we should start asserting more boldly that you *can* know Christ's disciples by their fruits, and they point overwhelmingly back to Rome.

So while I still am frustrated occasionally by the extreme worldliness, craven cowardice, and wildly misplaced priorities of many Catholics and church leaders (to say nothing of the outright crimes that have been committed or covered up), I no longer doubt. The church has survived such saboteurs before. The faith, the sacraments, and many holy priests and bishops are all there. A faithful Catholic life is within reach of each one of us. (And may we who justly grumble against these occasional outrages beware lest we ourselves become occasions for stumbling.)

I broke off my discernment with Orthodoxy amicably. A six-month-long relationship was also coming to an end now, but I continued driving to Nashville on the weekends. I drove a '95 Volvo 960, a surprisingly dependable old beater Alice had sold me while in seminary. Over time multiple systems had broken down: inside door panels had been torn off so that a mass of wires hung next to my passenger's lap, and the door frame metal itself had to be grasped to enable opening and shutting. I viewed the car as a good test for whatever girl I'd date. Surely I'd weed out the gold diggers this way.

One advantage to staying Catholic was the exploding young adult population in Nashville. With nearly a decade of community under my belt, I had no trouble finding groups to hang out with and parties to frequent. It was at one such party that I met a very British-looking gal who I sidled on up to and struck up a conversation with. She had ivory-looking skin and brown hair, but beyond that (my type) she also was the spitting image of Emilia Clarke. I'm not a *Game of Thrones* fan, but I know a girl with movie-star good looks when I see one. I immediately sensed as well that there was more to her than looks. Our conversation took a turn fairly quickly to liturgy, and I learned she was a member of St. Mary of the Seven Sorrows parish in Downtown Nashville, the oldest standing church in the city, and home to the most gorgeous Novus Ordo celebration of the Mass this side of St. John Cantius in Chicago. Our conversation was brief (as all first conversations should be), but I was keeping copious mental notes.

I did some recon with Alice, who'd actually known Maude (her name) for years. Maude's grandfather was a noted Southern author (Madison Jones) and her dad had passed away the same year I'd become Catholic. And she was in St. Mary's choir with Alice; would I like her to tell Maude I'd asked about her? Sure, I said—and I knew what church I'd be attending Sunday.

She looked genuinely pleased to see me after Mass when I walked up to her. Luckily, she and the other choir members invited me to coffee down the street, and so I had ample time to get her phone number.

Maude was cautious, the opposite of me. I had to move slower with her than any previous girl, and at one point I wasn't sure she wanted to get engaged. But after a bit more preparation, she said yes, and we began planning our wedding. It was to be at St. Mary's of course, with our good friend and now pastor Father Jayd Neely celebrating. Maude worked part time for him as bookkeeper of the parish, and so I got to know him and the choir director, Dr. Nancy Sutton, well.

Third time's a charm, and with head, heart, and soul finally lined up since I'd found Maude, she became my wife in the summer of 2020. This was during the COVID-19 pandemic, which delayed us from our initial date in April. But it worked out, because when we did get married, the restrictions had eased somewhat. We had to trade our dream Prague honeymoon for one in the Smokies and western North Carolina, but all in all it felt right. Lockdown and masks would return shortly after we settled into married life, however.

And settled we have, of a sort: our son was born a little over a year after we wed. My first-born son, as I said at the outset, was born in the same hospital tower that I was, only now it bore a Catholic name. He soon did as well, when he was baptized in the name of the Holy Trinity a couple weeks later by Father Neely.

His life will be different than mine in a few important ways. My travels, physically, mentally, and spiritually, have brought me, after much turbulence, to a settled-ness in this world that I could've never predicted for that young, anxious, confused Jehovah's Witness boy. Though bereft at birth of much, little by little God has led me along the path of rediscovery. First, in his truth—the truth about him, his workings and ways in the world, and finally his church and sacraments. But from this other goods have flowed.

I have a country. I can tear up now during the national anthem at a football game. Again, that's separate from politics. My patriotism isn't dependent on that. Rather, it's about loving a place, a people, and a story. The history, the language, the land, the food, the culture, the familiarity—today I choose to love these things as parts of my very self and of those I love. That leads to identity. As a Witness, you have one identity, and that is Witness. You're a foreigner in your native land because the only attachment you're allowed is to the ever-changing diktats of Watchtower. As a Catholic, yes, my primary identity is "follower of Christ." But in Catholicism, the universal does not destroy the particular. Universal truths are embodied in the particular. In fact, in an Aristotelian sense, their existence is solely in the particular. We venerate holy sites and people and relics in Catholicism because God showed us the hallowed possibilities of the specific when he came in a certain flesh at a certain time and place.

Our time and place, all the actions God allows, either actively or passively, are part of the unfolding epic of salvation. The place your great-great-great grandfather is buried, the ring your grandmother wore, the factory your dad worked at—these are the sacred spaces and relics of your lineage, which is an essential chapter in the story God is weaving. We ought to be passionately attached to these things and accord them the reverence they deserve as intentions of the providential Sacred Heart.

But the modern world, the thing birthed by the Enlightenment, seeks to belittle and destroy all this. It disenchants whereas Catholicism imbues with meaning and significance. The place where you took your first breath—according to modernism, it's just a commodity, something you can trade away when you outgrow. Your town, your state, even your friends—these are ultimately interchangeable cogs in an economic wheel that ceaselessly shuffles us around in the single-minded pursuit of profit. You can bet I'm for reducing the GDP, if that means more stability, more constancy, and greater reverence for what matters. My childen may brush all this off as the ravings of an eccentric old man one day, but they will at least be brought up to understand this precious birthright. They will be instructed on the spiritual value of inhabiting the places their ancestors haunt.

Because we've become so enamored with the spirit of this reductionist, rationalizing world rather than the world our fathers knew, we've abandoned much of our common religious imagination. Do you know of the traditional beliefs surrounding Halloween? How the veil between this life and the next thins that night, in preparation for our enhanced communion with God's saints the next day, such that souls in purgatory many times return to the places they lived on that eve? Light a candle, for this reminds them of the purgative fire of Christ's love, which is the only path to the joy of heaven that they seek. Or did you know that the dew that covers the grass on Pentecost morning has healing properties ("Heal our wounds, our strength renew; on our dryness pour thy dew"[5]), and that a barefoot walk outside on that blessed morn might do you good? These are the beliefs we've forgotten, and with them are a whole host of traditions and practices which we've lost that concretize the grace of the liturgical year and enchant the days with the beauty of our faith.

We don't have to get rid of the internet or air conditioning to restore our traditional beliefs and culture. Ludditism is a dead end and a distraction. I as much as anyone want to live with modern convenience and comfort. The trick is to not let this comfortable world dull to the point where it doesn't seem worth living in.

We've physically incarnated so much ugly scientism into our society. We build for the personal automobile so that we can zip from parking lot to

---

5. From the *Veni Creator Spiritus* sequence.

parking lot and miss the wonderful granularity of every inch of our world. We construct our new civic landmarks—our office and condo towers—out of cold steel, glass, and concrete, having not even the decency to adorn their nakedness with designs or intricacies which could soften them. Their angular assaults on our psyches are celebrated by a brainwashed clique of architects who view the saner tastes of the common people with elitist disdain. And every settled form, folkway, and familiarity could at any moment be smashed and consigned to the flames in the name of "progress."

My study of philosophy has led me to the postmodernists—Lyotard, Derrida, and Foucault, among others. Their ruthlessly consistent deconstruction of Western Modernism and Enlightenment Rationalism provides the raw material from which a better world could be built atop the ashes of these bankrupt ideologies. Their insight is basically that the Enlightenment's destruction of Christendom and all traditional cultures was nothing more than an imperialistic switcheroo. Sure, it got one thing dead-on, the material sciences and technology, but its metaphysics (which it foolishly believes it doesn't have) were just as faith-based as any "primitive" belief system. It turns out it's actually faith all the way down, and that a Kierkegaardian "leap" is required of all of us, not just Christians.

My children will grow up amidst the seasonal rhythms of the liturgical year, marking the sacred movements of time. They'll grow up in an enchanted, spirit-haunted world, imbued with meaning and significance because the God who is upholding it requires such by his very nature. And they'll understand their place in it: the great men and women of their nation who wrote its story, and the great men and women of their own lineage who made them part of that story. That lineage is playing itself out in their particular neighborhood and its institutions. They will see their crucial roles in those structures because we will teach them the joy of civic engagement, of volunteering, and of being both physically and emotionally invested in the people that walk about on the same hallowed ground as they do. They will have not only the fullness of the faith, but also the fullness of life which flows from that faith.

One thing it appears they won't have, and which I have no power to give them, is a normal relationship with their paternal grandparents. I'll end my story by describing the situation as it stands. At each major life event, I've half-consciously hoped that there would be some change in my parents' stance toward me. We recently passed the ten-year mark since that bleak day when I told my parents I was Catholic and that I was leaving for boot camp the next morning. Throughout that long span of little more than sporadic, surface-level communication of necessary family business, when I've had to explain the situation to people unfamiliar with Jehovah's Witnesses, they've sympathized and then kindly reassured me with something like, "I know that's hard, but I knew a fellow who converted from (insert Evangelical Protestant group), and his parents didn't talk to him for years, but eventually they softened and now things are basically back to normal."

While well-intentioned, such anecdotes really aren't analogous to this situation at all. My parents love me and my family and deeply enjoy our company. Ever since my tumultuous teenage years, I've gotten along great with my parents and sister. There's no natural friction here, even with the difference in beliefs—in fact, I think my dad would be curious about my beliefs if left to his own devices. What has prolonged this shunning and what will continue to prolong it is outside enforcement. The bottom line is that my parents aren't allowed to have a relationship with me, even if everything within them on a natural level desires it. Even if we agreed to never discuss religion or worldviews, I am a danger to their faith and their whole social life simply by existing as a Catholic. No exceptions.

Sometimes now I do feel a certain enmity between us that wasn't there in the beginning. It's gotten harder to accept what they're doing, not easier, and I think that's because the longer it goes on, the more I can't believe they're actually doing it. To shun for a year or two to try to "wake someone up" from a certain behavior—I don't agree with it, but it's almost understandable. To go ten years and counting, and to say as Dad explicitly told me, that he's ready to go to his grave unreconciled, is difficult to comprehend. I'd be lying if I said watching the years slowly slip away has not allowed bitterness to seep in.

Maude and I have struggled to understand the unwritten rules that govern JW shunning. The one or two cracks in the dam that have momentarily given us hope have been quickly repaired, leaving us baffled as to what may be happening behind the scenes. I understand it must be tough for them: how do you have a relationship with your daughter-in-law and grandchildren while keeping your distance from your son? Watchtower gives them rules, but how difficult they must be to apply in such a complicated situation!

And what boundaries should we set? Do we allow them to determine the parameters of the relationship, taking what we can get, or do we issue an ultimatum? I believe, though, that such a condition would only make their grim business easier and push them toward a clean break. I want my children to know their grandparents. I'm glad I knew mine, despite whatever flaws they may have had.

On a spiritual level, I've gradually been led to an awareness that this is actually a great opportunity for me. It seems that generally someone responding to Christ's call to "hate," or to not be unduly attached to his father, mother, and sister, isn't called to do so in such a literal way (Luke 14:26). Most parents don't oppose conversions to Catholicism anymore. But the vicissitudes of history have resulted in my card being pulled to drink the fullness of that verse to its dregs. Like a soldier or consecrated virgin before Caesar, my only escape from this fate is apostasy. I should thank God. Rarely is it so clear which path he desires for us.

I'm also lucky because this trial is the most purely Christ-like one I've ever born. The vast majority of my suffering has been due to my own sins: my hang-ups, inordinate desires, past mistakes, etc. When offered to God in union with Christ's sacrifice, such suffering is certainly efficacious. But even though we should avoid trying to map these things out like a math equation, there is a sense in which they fall under the heading of satisfaction—a making up for the lack in me, purging and refining me in this life, if I let it, rather than in Purgatory, God willing.

The gratuitous nature of the suffering imposed by the Jehovah's Witnesses, however, seems different. As guilty as I am in so many areas of life, here, I was literally born into this predicament. And when God reached into the whirlpool and drew me out, the light at the end of the tunnel was partially lit by a ring of fire. The fire is the one set by William Sheehan (later Shane) over 220 years ago when he abandoned his Catholic faith in the Virginia backwoods. I don't know why exactly, and I don't even blame him really, with the situation as it was for Catholics at the time, but that action severed our family from the living stream of truth until AD 2010. During that time, across the vast expanse of this country and down the generations, my forebears, themselves driven by the crushing disappointments of life, by confusion, ignorance, their own failings—but also by a desire for God, for righteousness and justice, and for clarity—embraced that particularly American Protestant sect, the Jehovah's Witnesses.

It's been all downhill since then, for the most part, though the "separateness" the Witnesses engender does lend itself to certain higher standards among its adherents (for cleanliness, for example, or their more dignified bearing, which is probably something common to many small, disciplined, exclusive groups). But theologically, they're further from the truth than almost all other Protestants. Many would not consider them Christian. It's a fact, then, that my family had wandered farther afield, had become more confused than most. The path back would correspondingly be harder and more convoluted. Like a rod bent far out of shape, it would take more force, more trauma, to get something like that straight again.

Someone had to pay that price. Like the cash infusions necessary to dig someone out of debt, the burn that exercise puts into stiff limbs, or the pangs of withdrawal when an addiction is kicked, in no scenario of this life is wrong put right without blood, sweat, and tears. This is so metaphysically true that it took literal blood, sweat, and tears to save the cosmos. The distance from where we'd fallen to where we needed to be was bridged by a divine sacrificial overstretching. It took the shape of a cross.

But as St. Paul tells us, there's something lacking in this all-sufficient, overflowing, impeccable, and unrepeatable self-oblation (Colossians 1:24). That's the space God leaves for each one of us within it. "Come, follow me." On this side of the Eschaton, that's always going to look like that bloody, dusty, mournful scene on Calvary hill, to a greater or lesser extent. I love my father, my mother, and my sister, and I can't describe to you the joy I'd feel to be part of their lives again. And even though I've offered some theories or rationalizations for why this is all happening, in truth it remains an impenetrable mystery. Families as happy as ours shouldn't be separated like this.

But I'm equally convinced that my Divine Master, the one who chose me, my Eternal Father, has extended his hand to me. It took his work, his pain, to absorb the evil and right the universe, but it continues its saving power in our work, in this pain.

May I do my part in helping right the universe.

Appendix:
The Trinity for Jehovah's Witnesses

I've found that many arguments from Scripture for the Trinity don't get at the heart of the issue for Jehovah's Witnesses, or they can be dismissed as insufficiently clear. What follows are some of the texts that don't leave any room for doubt.

It's important to present it this way when speaking with a Witness: yes, Scripture portrays Christ and God the Father as separate persons, and Christ is always portrayed as "secondary" in a certain sense to the Father. Catholics will usually say this only applies to his humanity, but when they say this they're neglecting the "economic" (meaning something like the practical or functional) procession within the Trinity in which the Son comes from the Father. Begotten is the language used, and we clarify that in the Creed by saying "before all ages." So, yes, there's a sense in which the Father is "greater than" the Son, even in their coeternal, coequal divinity. But that second part cannot be ignored: Christ is the eternal, divine Son of God, not a created, angelic son of God.

If you can show the Witness that Trinitarianism is not arguing for a three-headed God, but that rather, there's a "monarchy" to God the Father (this is the term used in the East), then you've disarmed a lot of his criticism. He's going to reach immediately for statements by Our Lord like, "The Father is greater than I am" (John 14:28). Again, the stock Christian response of, "That's only in regard to his humanity," doesn't cut it with them. Why then is the resurrected, glorified Christ to become "subject" to the Father in the Eschaton? (1 Cor. 15:28). Obviously, the JW belief about the nature of Christ is catching a whiff of something real (the *economic* "subordination" of the Son to the Father, even apart from his humanity) and then distorting it beyond its limited meaning.

APPENDIX: THE TRINITY FOR JEHOVAH'S WITNESSES

The thing to get him to understand, though, is that with all this being conceded regarding the relation between Father and Son (and by extension Holy Ghost), we must square this with those Scriptures which admit of no other interpretation than that Christ is divine, and divine in the sense that first century Jews would've understood that term. The first chapter of Hebrews is the best exposition of Christ's divinity to show a Witness because it directly refutes the idea that Christ is an angel, which is what JWs explicitly believe (specifically, that he is Michael the Archangel). Perhaps even more undeniable is Colossians 2:9: the *"fullness* of deity dwells bodily" (emphasis mine) in Christ. Fullness of deity leaves no room for JW interpretation. The fullness of deity is only found in God. He also has the form of God (Philippians 2:6). Do angels have the form of God? Only by stretching that term to mean any kind of spiritual nature, in which case St. Paul could've said so ("the form of angels" or something).

John 1:1 is tricky because they mistranslate it. "In the beginning was the Word, and the Word was with God, and the Word was God." The actual Greek doesn't say "the" God or "a" god: it features a construction that means "divine," and in context clearly refers to the doctrine of the Trinity.[1] How could someone be both "with God" and "divine"? Only if there were multiple persons sharing one absolutely unique essence. (Jews believed God, and therefore his "essence," was absolutely unique.) His point is to say that Christ is the son of God, a person other than God, but that he is divine as only God is. The Trinity is the only possible explanation for the specific linguistic construction of that verse.

Finally, there are many places in the New Testament where the writers quote passages attributed to God in the Old Testament and apply them to Christ. Hebrews 1:10–12 ("Thou in the beginning, O Lord, didst found the earth: and the works of thy hands are the heavens") is very clearly taken from Psalm 101:26–28 ("O Lord, thou foundedst the earth: and the heavens are the works of thy hands"). Paul is saying, "This stuff you believe God did? Christ did it. Because Christ is also who God is." John does this in his gospel at 12:37–41, referring to the sixth chapter of Isaiah. John says Isaiah saw Jesus' "glory, and spoke of him." But Isaiah sets up the scene as Isaiah seeing God: "I saw the Lord sitting upon a throne high and elevated: and his train filled the temple."

---

1. Harner, "Qualitative Anarthrous Predicate Nouns."

Bibliography

Bradshaw, David. *Aristotle East and West: Metaphysics and the Division of Christendom.* Cambridge University Press, 2007.

Bunge, Gabriel, OSB. *Earthen Vessels: The Practice of Personal Prayer According to the Patristic Tradition.* San Francisco: Ignatius, 2002.

Fortescue, Adrian. *The Early Papacy: To the Synod of Chalcedon in 451.* San Francisco: Ignatius, 2008.

Pope Francis. "Post-Synodal Apostolic Exhortation *Amoris Laetitia* of the Holy Father Francis to Bishops, Priests and Deacons, Consecrated Persons, Christian Married Couples, and All the Lay Faithful on Love in the Family." https://www.vatican.va/content/francesco/en/apost_exhortations/documents/papa-francesco_esortazione-ap_20160319_amoris-laetitia.html.

Grube, G.M.A., and Reeve, C.D.C. transl. Plato: *Republic*. In *Plato: Complete Works.* Edited by John M. Cooper and D.S. Hutchinson, 971–1223. Indianapolis: Hackett, 2010.

Harner, Philip B. "Qualitative Anarthrous Predicate Nouns: Mark 15:39 and John 1:1." *Journal of Biblical Literature* 92 (1973) 75–87. https://www.jstor.org/stable/3262756.

John Climacus. *The Ladder of Divine Ascent.* Translated by Archimandrite Lazarus Moore. Willits, CA: Eastern Orthodox, 1959.

Kreeft, Peter. *Fundamentals of the Faith: Essays in Christian Apologetics.* San Francisco: Ignatius, 1998.

Kuyper, Abraham. *Lectures on Calvinism.* New York: Cosimo Classics, 2007.

Lavaca Collective. *Sin Patrón: Stories from Argentina's Worker-Run Factories.* Chicago: Haymarket, 2007.

Lewis, C. S. *Mere Christianity.* New York: HarperCollins, 2001.

McDowell, Josh and Sean. *More Than a Carpenter.* Carol Stream, IL: Tyndale Elevate, 2009.

Pulkkanen, Johannes. "The Dark Night: St John of the Cross and Eastern Orthodox Theology." PhD diss., Uppsala University, 2009.

Spurlock, Morgan, director. *Super Size Me.* Sony Pictures, 2004.

Stott, John. *Becoming a Christian.* Westmont, IL: IVP, 1951.

Strobel, Lee. *The Case for Christ: A Journalist's Personal Investigation of the Evidence for Jesus.* Grand Rapids: Zondervan, 2002.

Wright, N.T. *The Resurrection of the Son of God (Christian Origins and the Question of God, Vol. 3).* Minneapolis: Fortress, 2003.

www.ingramcontent.com/pod-product-compliance
Lightning Source LLC
Chambersburg PA
CBHW050823160426
43192CB00010B/1875